practical CLASSICS

on Colour MGB GT Restoration

Published by
KELSEY PUBLISHING LTD

Published by Kelsey Publishing Ltd
Printed in the UK by CBE 2000 Ltd
on behalf of Kelsey Publishing Ltd,
Kelsey House, 77 High Street, Beckenham,
BR3 1AN (Tel: 0181-658 3531).

© 1996
ISBN 1873098 41 3

Acknowledgments

Our thanks to The MGB Hive for letting Peter Simpson 'look over their shoulders' and also to Peter
for covering the subject so thoroughly.
Finally our appreciation to Mark Dixon for the front cover photograph.

Contents

Introduction

Since 1980 *Practical Classics* has run no fewer than four full MGB rebuilds - hardly surprising when you consider just how popular the 'B' in all its forms is. However the project that this compilation is based on was our first GT, and the first time that we've covered any MGB project from beginning to end in colour throughout.

As Editor of *Practical Classics* from 1989 to 1994 I initiated and set up the MGB GT project. But shortly after the first episode appeared in print I was offered another position which was just too good to turn down and left *Practical Classics* full-time. However my successor John Pearson kindly asked me to complete the series in a freelance capacity.

We started in September 1994 with a very rusty GT that the MGB Hive bought in for, I believe, around £350. I then followed their progress as, over the following two years, they transformed it into, well, we weren't setting out to create a concours winner, but I reckon the vehicle that emerged wasn't far off!

Everything the most down-at-heel MGB is likely to need is covered, from refurbishing the shell (including new sills, floorpans, castle sections etc and repairing inner wings), through to fitting new outer panels, overhauling the engine, gearbox, front suspension and brakes, refitting the interior and the long-but-important process of fitting everything back up together. All these jobs (and many more) are covered in full detail in the pages that follow.

Over the years live followed quite a few restorations for magazines, and I have to say that The MGB Hive team who worked on this project are among the best I've worked with. Special mention must go to Neil Fincham who has to be one of the most skilled welders/fabricators in the business, and Norman Hatcher, whose engine and gearbox building ability must be seen to be believed!

It only remains for me to say that I hope you enjoy reading our first full-colour MGB restoration compilation as much as I enjoyed producing the material that comprises it.

Peter Simpson
Editor: *Car Mechanics*

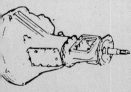

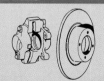

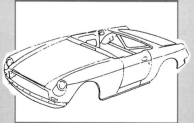

Project MGB

Once again we're setting off on the restoration trail - this time with an MGB GT. Peter Simpson introduces the car which will be giving us, and the restorers, hours of fun over the next few months.

We decided, after much long and hard thought, and numerous discussions, that it was time Practical Classics tackled an MGB restoration again. Yes, I know we've done them before. But believe it or not, it's now 12 (yes 12) years since we last covered rebuilding a rusty MGB. And restoration techniques, parts availability and the type of equipment available in home workshops have all changed immeasurably since then!

And you can't get away from it, MGBs are very popular. The majority of the MG Owners Club's 50,000 members own Bs, and the dozens of MGB specialists up and down the country just wouldn't exist if there wasn't a big demand for the parts and services they supply.

Choosing a car

Although MGBs are, shall we say, 'somewhat plentiful', we weren't just looking for any old rusty B. We needed something special. Our restoration projects have to have a good selection of typical faults - the more of them the better. This is so that we can demonstrate as many typical repair techniques as possible. A car that's spotless in one or more areas where most are weak may be an enthusiast's dream. But it's not much use to us.

On the other hand we're not after an absolute rot box either - a car that's so awful that no-one in their right mind would ever consider restoring it. For example, there's no point in us showing how to replace, say, a complete inner wing panel, if most cars need only an arch repair section.

Nice, isn't it! This is our latest restoration project - what have we done? The missing front wing is with the car, but both wings are rotten and will be replaced.

This is a very common MGB problem but hard to check for as it's normally covered by the front wing. It's the sill front closing panel, which is very important structurally, because it's what gives the sill box section much of its strength. The whole sill structure on both sides will need replacing - quite usual on rusty Bs.

All this is particularly relevant to MGBs, because parts availability is so good. I'm not talking just about the Heritage bodyshell. You can get every body panel new so it's rarely worth doing much in the way of repair work. Who is going to bother making and fitting front wing repair sections, when you can get a complete new wing for around £100?

Normally, when there's open and closed versions of a particular car, we go for the convertible. This is partly because it'll be worth more at the end, and project car restorations are expensive! More importantly though, while almost all the techniques involved in restoring a saloon can be demonstrated equally well on a convertible, a saloon rebuild won't usually include everything a convertible owner needs. On this occasion however we decided to cover the closed GT version, partly because our previous rebuild was a roadster, but also because there are some specific rot spots around the rear end of a GT - rectification of which we need to cover.

So we popped down to our local MGB specialists, the MGB Hive at Parson's Drove near Wisbech (0945 700500), where owners Nigel and Sandra Petch showed us some of the cars they have for restoration. The Hive has been trading for some 12 years, and as well as undertaking any MGB repair from routine servicing to full rebuilds (all for fixed quotes), they supply new and secondhand parts. They are MG Owners Club five-star and five-spanner approved specialists. The Hive also buy Bs for breaking and restoration, and restore cars for resale.

We looked at quite a few of the cars awaiting restoration or breaking in the field behind their

Another common problem-area, which can be seen only with the front wings off is the inner wing support/trumpet section. This should be a closed box section, but more usually it's open, like this!

There's rot in the screen pillar/surrounds too. From experience, I know that if a little rot is visible, there will be a lot more underneath! Localised repair may be just possible, but somehow I doubt it...

premises. A number were possibilities, but eventually we settled on COH 500K, a red 1971 BGT, which the MGB Hive are going to restore for us. As you can see, the car looks really awful, but underneath all that

matt, faded paintwork the car is... well, I can't go as far as to say it's 'surprisingly sound', but it certainly isn't as bad as I'd expected! The pictures show most of the problem areas which are apparent now, though I'm

he engine bay isn't at all bad for a project car. When bought COH 00K was a runner - it still would be if someone hadn't swiped the atteries! The engine is to be fully rebuilt.

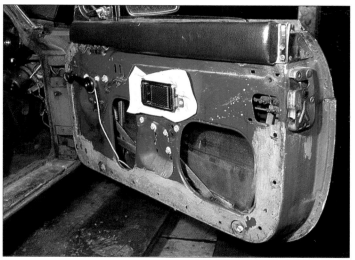

Now I might be wrong, but I've a funny feeling that driver's door might just be secondhand! The frame seems sound, but the skin at least will require replacing.

Project MGB

sure that one or two unexpected nasties will show up as we dig deeper!

What we got

The paintwork is something of a mystery. As well as the flat finish, the whole surface is crazed and cracked, and rust seems to be starting

underneath the cracks in some places, suggesting that the cracking goes right down to the base metal. Quite what's caused it we're not sure - it may be a reaction between incompatible paint types, or simply that too much paint has been applied and it's cracked during the drying-out process. But whatever's caused it there's only one solution - strip the whole lot right back to the bare metal, and start again.

The sills have been 'repaired' before (the panel gaps between sill and rear wings have been filled). There's plenty of rust in the rear wings too, though the inner arches don't look too bad. Both these are common MGB weak spots, and fitting new rear wings to a GT is somewhat different from doing the same job on a roadster.

Underneath she isn't too bad, although I'm sure some problems will emerge once we start cleaning things up properly - the back rear spring mounts look

dodgy, and work is definitely needed on the rear valance.

Mechanically the car doesn't seem too bad - it was a runner when bought. A rebuilt engine will however be fitted as a matter of course, and most of the underbonnet ancilliaries will also be replaced with rebuilt items. The transmission will be rebuilt if necessary, though it seems good.

The interior, on the other hand is quite definitely anything but good! No, let's not beat about the bush - it's awful! The seats are ripped to shreds, carpets virtually non-existent, and the side trim panels dirty, warped and damaged. I doubt if anything in there is worth saving. Fortunately, original-type MGB trim is readily available...

So there it is. Next month, we'll begin the restoration proper by stripping out the final remains of the interior, and starting to make the car structurally sound again. ∎

The passenger door needs frame work too. A complete new panel will probably be the most cost-effective solution here, and we may well end up replacing both doors.

The floor pans are pretty good, apart from along their outer edges where angle-pieces have been welded in, probably at the same time as the sills were repaired.

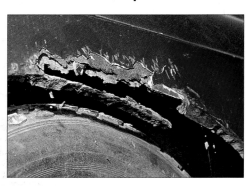

Both rear wings are write-offs - there's rot around the arches, in the front bottom corner and along the top joint. Both will need to be replaced. The rear wing's bottom corner has to come off anyway, to repair the sills properly.

The rear valance shows typical signs of bodged filler-repairs and rust breaking back through filler that's been applied over it. Often this rot spreads to the back rear spring mounting points in the chassis. Very dangerous, and a common MoT failure point!

Some interesting repair work around the luggage compartment! I just hope they removed that petrol tank first!

What a lovely sight! Somehow, I don't think there's much in here that can be salvaged!

RESTORATION PROJECT
1971
MGB

Work has started on our latest project car restoration. Peter Simpson covers the start of stripping the GT model and front wing removal.

Appearances can be deceptive. With its flat, crazed paintwork, missing front wing and disintegrating interior, our new project MGB GT looks to the untrained eye like a car with just one more journey ahead of it - to the scrapyard.

However, as our in-depth inspection last month suggested, it's not that bad once you look beyond the initial tattiness. In fact it's quite sound - in a 'needing restoration' kind of way!

So, having satisfied ourselves that the car was worth doing something with, it was time for some real work!

Be methodical

This is the key to successful dismantling. Don't, whatever you do, rush at the car, hyperactive socket set in hand, and remove anything and everything that will come off. Do that, and chances are you'll end up with a huge pile of bits of assorted shapes and sizes, but little idea how it all goes back together. However simple, straightforward and obvious the order of reassembly seems when you're dismantling, it will be anything but obvious when, possibly several months later, it's time to reassemble. I know. I've done it!

Think too whether everything really needs to come off at once. It's often better to tackle the car a bit at a time, and unless you're setting out to produce a concours car it's rarely necessary to remove everything. Our restorers (The MGB Hive, tel: 0945 700500), usually leave the engine and gearbox in place until the structural work is finished. It's simpler, and the engine's weight acting down also helps keep the shell in shape while the sills are chopped away. They also leave in the headlining and dash (both are awkward to remove and refit) unless they need attention.

Once you've decided what needs to come off, and what can be left in place, it's time to start planning. I recommend equipping

Right: In she comes! Our MGB being manhandled into the workshop so the pre-restoration stripdown can begin

2 ...and the seats can then be lifted out. They'll be refurbished later. Remove the rest of the soft trim (carpets, trim panels etc.) at this stage too. In our case there wasn't much of it left anyway - thankfully new MGB trim is readily available.

1 Front seats are removed complete with their runners. Two bolts hold each runner to the floor...

5 The grille is held on by six screws - three at the top and three at the bottom, the latter being covered by rubber bungs. It can then be lifted up and away.

6 Neil then removed the front bumper. It's far easier to undo the bolts holding the bumper irons onto the chassis (two on each side), and then pull the bumper off with its irons still attached.

7 The decks are now almost clear for the front wings to come off. Neil first undid the two bolts down the front, just behind the grille aperture. Most of the wing securing bolts screw into captive nuts in the wing - sometimes a little penetrating oil or WD40 helps the removal process!

3 Neil reckons it's easiest to remove headlamps before taking a front wing off. Prise the headlamp rim off and then undo the three cross-head screws holding the lamp securing ring. The headlamp sealed-beam unit can then be unplugged. If the headlamp bowl is worth saving it can be unscrewed from the wing, but few are worth it.

4 Next the wires between the wing and body are disconnected - simply pull the Lucar connectors apart.

8 Next, Neil undid the long row of bolts along the wing's top edge. Note that a couple of them go into loose (not captive) nuts and also hold the bonnet release mechanism, so a second spanner is needed.

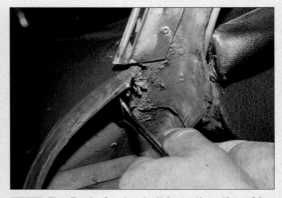

9 The final wing-top bolt is on the other side of the wing, in the top corner, pointing inwards. You can reach it only with the door open.

Project MGB

yourself with several stout cardboard boxes and a quantity of polythene money bags - get some from your bank. The latter are for storing related small components, such as washers, spacers, nuts, bolts etc. They're sturdy, easy to seal, and some even have a handy white area on which you can write what's inside!

The boxes can then be used to store components that go together - a seat and its mountings for example. Masking tape is very useful for holding related pieces together - a fitting and its bolts, washers, locking tabs etc. for example, and again, you can write on the tape what the parts are, and where they go.

It's also often possible to refit nuts and bolts to something once it's been taken off the car - which of course means you can also refit all the spacers and washers in exactly the same order as you took them off. Never, ever trust your memory on things like this. Pencil-sketches or, better still, photographs of things coming apart are also useful.

Parts books

Don't, however, assume that the car was 100% right when you started work. Most old cars have been tinkered with at some time, and someone else may have got it wrong. Get hold of a factory parts book if you can.

Unlike workshop manuals (even factory ones), which show only what you take apart for service or overhaul purposes, parts books show every single component (including the ones which normally aren't touched once a car's been built) and the order of assembly.

All this may sound like an unneccessary chore, but believe me, it can and will save you time, hassle and (if you lose anything, which you probably will otherwise) money in the long run. In this context, remember that parts which don't normally deteriorate or wear out in service (in other words ones which won't

need replacing unless someone loses them!) are often very hard to find.

Not many people stock things like heater ducts, dashboard support brackets, seat runners, complete hinges etc. because, in the normal way, they never need replacing.

The pictures show how Neil at the MGB Hive started taking our car apart. The main job undertaken this month was front wing removal. Theoretically, this is a relatively straightforward nuts and bolts job. In practice, on our car it wasn't quite that simple. As you'll see...

NEXT MONTH Removing glas exterior brightwo lights and petro tank

10 Finally, there's a vertical row of bolts inside the car, under the dash. On the nearside these can all be reached quite easily once you've taken the glovebox interior out. However to reach the offside ones you have to unbolt the wiper motor. It also helps if you take the fuel gauge out.

11 Theoretically, you should then be able to lift the wing off after removing three small screws along the bottom edge. Not in our case though. A previous repairer had welded the lower edge and sill bottom together. So out came the air-chisel (tinsnips would have done as well), which sliced straight through the bottom edge as if it was cutting paper...

12 The wing could then be lifted off and away. Note that the side/indicator lamp unit is still attached. That's because ours wasn't reusable, so it accompanied the wing onto the scrap metal pile.

13 This is the remains of the sill closing section, open for all to see once the front wing was removed. No wonder the chisel cut through it so easily - apart from the wing itself, it was cutting through air!

1971 MGB

Work on our latest project car continues with some more stripping-out. Peter Simpson reports on removing glass, lights, trim and the petrol tank.

Last month, we started removing the 'peripherals' from our 1971 MGB GT shell, and got as far as taking the remaining front wing off. Then, after taking the windscreen wipers/washers and screen out, attention moved to the back of the car...

As the pictures show, all this work is fairly basic and straightforward 'nuts and bolts' stuff. And how much care you take over some aspects will probably depend how much of the car you want to (or is fit to!) re-use.

However the MGB Hive's procedures are a very useful guide in this respect because our car is being restored for resale. So while anything that needs replacing clearly will be, there's an incentive to re-use parts that can be refurbished.

This is good from a coverage point of view too. MGB owners have truly unrivalled parts back-up, and can often obtain replacement parts which owners of other models can only dream about. As this project continues, we may well refurbish a few things which could be replaced instead - so that non-MGB owners derive some extra benefit from the series.

Take it steady

It's worth repeating a couple of the points I made last month, for the benefit of new readers.

First, don't pull everything off the car and pile it up in the corner of the garage. Store the parts sensibly and tidily. However straightforward and logical the order of assembly looks now, it'll be a completely different story when you come to reassemble. Especially if that's several months later and/or you've managed to lose a couple of vital bits in the meantime!

Secondly, make notes and sketches and, if you can, take a few photographs. As well as aiding your memory, some decent before and during restoration photographs will be needed when you submit your finished rebuild story to Practical Classics! Masking tape is a great help for keeping related items together and freezer labels can be used for identification.

It's also a good idea, where possible, to loosely reassemble

REMOVING WIPERS, GLASS AND LIGHTS

1 Windscreen wiper spindle nuts rarely unscrew, so drastic measures are called for. This is the MGB Hive's recommended approach. Saw across the flats like this....

2 ...and then knock the remaining section of the nut around. It will spread slightly in the process, which makes it easier to knock off.

3 To get the wiper rack out, you need to push the two heater vents out, and disconnect all the associated piping. This also gives access to the washer assembly, which pushes up and out from inside.

7 Then he tackled the front hinged section on the back of the door pillar...

8 ...and the glass, complete with its frame, was lifted out.

9 The bright strip around the roof gutter is riveted on. To remove, you drill throught the rivets. It's easy to inadvertently scratch or mark the strip - stop the drill as soon as the rivet head disappears.

Flashback to last month when we started work on our tatty, non-running GT. Binding brakes and squashy tyres make a car much harder to push!

4 It's quite hard to extract the inset bright trim from an MGB screen rubber without damaging it, and the trim is hard to reshape once it's twisted. If the rubbers are past their best (most are) you can simply cut through them, releasing the strip and glass. New rubbers for MGBs are, of course, readily available.

5 When the windscreen is released from the rubber it can be lifted out. Be careful - MGBs have laminated windscreens which are much more fragile than toughened ones. Make sure the glass is completely free. Then lift it evenly and without distorting. Unlike metal, glass won't bend. It's also heavier than you might expect, and I'd definitely wear gloves.

6 Turning now to the side windows, to remove these Neil first unscrewed the rear catches from the rear screen pillar.

10 The strip can then be lifted off. It comes away in two pieces, the join being just above the centre pillar.

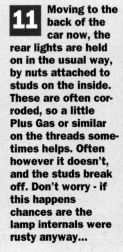

11 Moving to the back of the car now, the rear lights are held on in the usual way, by nuts attached to studs on the inside. These are often corroded, so a little Plus Gas or similar on the threads sometimes helps. Often however it doesn't, and the studs break off. Don't worry - if this happens chances are the lamp internals were rusty anyway...

12 The lamp unit will then lift out. The wires should be unplugged at the 'Lucar' plug-connectors a little way down.

Project MGB

things, in the order that they came off. If, for example, you've taken off a hinge that's held on by four nuts and bolts, each with a spacer, washer and spring washer, put everything back on the bolts in the order that they came off. Then refit the nuts. An instant ready-reference to what should go where!

Also, if (like me) you're the sort of person who loses things,

you're much less likely to lose one big lump than several small ones!

Fuel tank removal

As we're covering petrol tank removal, a few safety warnings are needed. First, and most obvious, don't forget to drain the tank before you remove it! However even a drained tank will retain some petrol vapour, and petrol vapour is highly inflammable, even in tiny quantities. So take care! The battery should of course be disconnected, but take it out of the workshop too.

Also avoid doing anything that could create sparks. So don't use heat, or a grinder to remove stubborn nuts and bolts.

Then, when the tank is out,

store it well away from the car - not in the same workshop. In fact I usually take petrol tanks outside. Choose somewhere sheltered though, so that rainwater or moisture cannot get inside.

All this may sound a bit excessive, but believe me, just one spark could set your whole garage alight. With you inside. Ask a fireman if you don't believe me!

Next month, with the shell

fully stripped, we'll start on the serious restoration work. The first job will be to chop out the rotten nearside sill assembly. We'll probably also need to remove some of the floorpan, and depending how bad it is, we may well have to take out the whole floor out before we reach solid metal.

NEXT MONTH Sill removal

13 The reversing lamps are secured, and removed, in the same way.

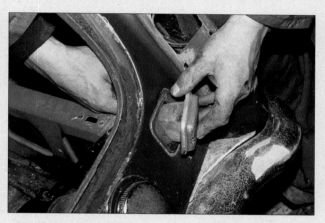

14 As mentioned when we took the front bumper off last month, it's usually best to remove the bumpers complete with their mounting irons. This is one of the two rear mounting bolts. Again, they're often very tight, and a little lubricant helps.

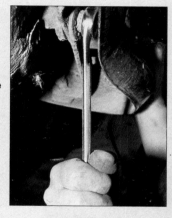

15 Taking off the rear bumper revealed a very fragile rear valance indeed. It consisted of rust, filler and thick paint in roughly equal quantities!

16 The petrol tank is below the floor. This fixing arrangement is not original, there should be nuts welded into the boot floor and bolts through the tank into them from underneath, as well as some bolts going through into semi-captive nuts from on top. To remove the tank, undo the bolts from underneath first. Don't forget to empty the tank!

17 Next, after disconnecting the fuel feed line (cut through it and fit a new one on rebuilding unless it's perfect), remove the fuel filler pipe by undoing both clips. Then place a trolley jack underneath the tank, undo the top bolts...

18 ...and the tank can be lowered down and back. Store it well away from where you're working on the car - the smallest residue of petrol vapour is highly inflammable!

MGB

AS WITH unitary construction cars, an MGB relies on its sills to give the shell its strength. The sills hold the front and rear of the car together, so it's important that they're sound.

But the trouble is, they're also very prone to corrosion, and you can be sure that the MoT tester will give this part of your car a very thorough inspection. If he thinks they've been weakened by corrosion, your car will fail.

Thankfully, MGB sill structures are more substantial than most. There are four pieces of metal running the whole length as double box sections, which flatten to form wedge-shaped sections at each end, under the front and rear wings.

The inner box is effectively closed by a square panel, the front one forming part of the front bulkhead and the rear, part of the inner wheelarch. Thus you have a closed double box section which, as long as all its component parts are present and sound, will remain rigid. Unfortunately that's not usually the case with most tired MGBs.

Much of this structure is hidden. With the car complete, all you can see are the centre of the outer sill, the floor-to-doorstep sill, the door shut and, if you crawl or feel underneath, the centre of the castle section. You can only see the outer surface of these parts.

Double trouble

This is a problem on two counts. Firstly, because rusting usually starts from the inside of a box-section, you won't know anything is wrong until holes appear in one of the visible external panels. By then, the tinworm will have eaten right through much of the unseen structure. So, long before you can see that anything's wrong, the basic structure will have been dangerously weakened.

> Peter Simpson covers the removal of the sill, floorpan and centre crossmember — work that will be needed on most rusty MGBs.

SILL, FLOORPAN AND CROSSMEMBER

1 First job is to remove the door. Theoretically an easy-enough job with a crosshead screwdriver. In practice though the setscrews are usually rock-tight, and some persuasion is required with an impact driver.

2 The sills go underneath the front and rear wings. Front wings are no problem as they bolt on. The rears have to be cut away at the lower edge like this. We'll be fitting complete rear wings, but you can get a repair section for this corner only.

3 Next, Neil attacked the outer sill by cutting along just in front of the lip, and then in from the outside. Note that the sill runs underneath the door pillar, so don't forget to remove this bit, and to clean up the fixing tabs, before trying to fit the new sill panel.

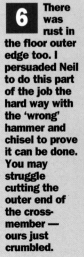

6 There was rust in the floor outer edge too. I persuaded Neil to do this part of the job the hard way with the 'wrong' hammer and chisel to prove it can be done. You may struggle cutting the outer end of the crossmember — ours just crumbled.

7 Now you need to separate the inner sill assembly from the bulkhead, again by cutting through the join. This is what you see from the outside...

8 ...and this is it from the inside. See now how cutting through the bulkhead freed the inner sill? All that's now holding this lump of rusty metal in place is the join between the castle section and the rear piece of the inner sill.

Neil Fincham, the MGB Hive's welder and fabricator, surrounded by the results of his labours. Note how the car is supported by axle stands under the front crossmember and rear axle. The scissor jack is there should any adjustment be needed.

4 With the outer sill freed all round, the next stage was easy — pull the outer sill down, and break it off at the bottom. Much of the centre membrane was non-existent, as expected, and the remainder could be separated from the inner sill and castle section easily.

5 Next job is to cut through the inner sill vertically, about 3in behind the centre crossmember, but in front of the corner reinforcing piece that runs over the rear of the inner sill.

9 At first we thought this would break as soon as the front piece was moved. However, a little more hammer and chisel work was needed before the rusty castle section finally parted company, allowing the whole assembly to be removed from the car.

10 This is what you'll be left with. The back piece of inner sill is left in position for now, as it has to be removed carefully so that the reinforcing member can be retained and reused.

1971 MGB

Secondly, the areas most susceptible to rot are the two ends of the sills, which are the two areas most comprehensively covered up.

Because of this, it's relatively simple to bodge a sill to pass an MoT test, either by cutting out the visible rust and welding in new metal, or by fixing plates or a cover sill over the affected areas. As long as the welding is up to scratch, and the metal that the new parts are attached to is sound, it will pass.

But don't be under any illusions, the sill won't be much stronger, and you certainly won't have stopped the rusting process. All you've done is covered, rather than cured the problem.

Fix it properly

So now we know why sills are so important, and why they rust. Hopefully, I've also persuaded you that cover sills aren't a good idea, and you want to know how to do the job properly.

The key is to cut out all the rusty metal, every bit of it, and replace it with new material, fitted in exactly the same way as it was by the factory. As you can see from the pictures, that involves cutting out and removing a lot of metal, since sill rot on MGBs usually leads to floorpan rot.

The centre crossmember usually needs replacing too. Although this comes as one piece, it's more convenient to replace it in two halves, as each side of the car is repaired. This involves cutting a new panel in half and then rewelding the two halves together on the car, but the join is right in the centre and can be made invisible and as strong as the original.

Many cars need bracing before you start cutting away at the sills, to stop them from distorting. However you don't have to worry too much about this on an MGB GT, because the sill structure is more substantial than most, and one sill, plus the stiffness added by the roof, will keep the car sufficiently in shape for the other sill to be replaced.

Carry out this work on a level floor. Support the car with four axle stands, two under the rear axle and two under the front crossmember. If you suspect the car may have sagged, which is most likely on a Roadster, check to see if the door gaps are roughly even, allowing for any hinge wear or drop.

Then take a scissor jack and, using a length of timber to spread the load, support the car under the floor with the jack. Don't take any weight on the jack as that will alter the position of everything when the sill is removed.

If the door gap test or anything else (like a new panel not fitting) suggests that the car has moved, you can then adjust the position before the new sill goes

SILL, FLOORPAN AND CROSSMEMBER continued

11 At this stage, if you haven't already done so, you should remove the exhaust. If it's in good condition, save it, otherwise just get it out of the way as quickly as possible without damaging the body mounts.

12 It's now time to attack the rest of the floorpan. First cut along this edge, just behind the crossmember, but taking care not to damage the securing tabs which are on the underside of the floorpan.

16 At this stage we weren't certain how much repair the leg would need, so Neil unscrewed the two bolts holding the gearbox crossmember on to the leg, after placing another jack and wooden block under the gearbox to take the weight.

17 Taking off the rest of the floor revealed a sound chassis leg, apart from the join with the crossmember, which will need some localised repair. When removing the floorpan, Neil cut about ½in in front of the join to allow for the transmission tunnel's tab underneath the floor.

THE MGB HIVE

This restoration is being carried out for us by the MGB Hive of Parson Drove, near Wisbech, Cambs (0945 700500). As well as being the region's leading supplier of MGB parts, the MGB Hive also undertakes all kinds of repair and restoration work, from routine servicing upwards. Cars are also restored for resale.

n by simply raising or lowering he scissor jack slightly.

Support the car like this and, o long as you don't take both ills off at the same time, you vill be okay.

Cutting out

s you may have spotted lready, this month's work nvolves a lot of metal cutting, nd I've showed Neil emonstrating an angle grinder nd cutting disc, air chisel and

(a little reluctantly) the hand chisel and hammer method.

If you're sufficiently masochistic you could do the whole job with a hammer and chisel. However it will take a very long time, and to be honest, if I was tackling a job this size, I'd invest $50 in an angle-grinder. As well as saving effort, angle grinders produce a much cleaner cut that requires little, if any, dressing afterwards. There are one or two corners on jobs like this that a

grinder can't reach, but you can do those by hand.

An air chisel, on the other hand, is something of a noisy luxury. They certainly make life easier if you already have compressed air, but I wouldn't recommend buying a complete air set-up just to do this job.

Plan what you're cutting out. When replacing a lot of interconnected panels you can often save time by taking several off in one lump as we have. But do keep in mind how far back you want to go, and make sure you leave enough original material for use as reference.

Fixing tabs are often found underneath panels you're replacing, but mustn't be cut off with them, as they are needed to attach the new panels.

As you can see from the picture sequence, the main sill structure (apart from the rear part of the inner sill, which we'll be dealing with next time) comes off in two pieces, one of them with a strip of floor attached. Then the rest of the floor comes out, but separately from the central crossmember which comes off last of all.

The chassis leg (running from the front of the car back under the floorpan) should be left intact, as it doesn't always have to be replaced. Sometimes, as in our case, it needs only localised repair, which is much easier.

NEXT ISSUE Preparing to fit new panels

13 Cut along the other two sides, again allowing for the tabs which extend underneath from the transmission tunnel, nd you can then remove the rear section of floor.

14 Now the piece of floor directly above the crossmember comes off. The best way is to cut along inside the crossmember, leaving the strip of floor directly above the crossmember's tabs in place. The crossmember is going to be replaced anyway.

15 Trim away the front floor outside the main chassis leg. Notice that Neil has now put the scissor jack underneath the chassis leg as an extra support.

18 Neil then removed the crossmember itself by sawing through the inboard edge. The join with the chassis leg needed very little encouragement to part, due to the amount of corrosion present.

19 Finally, Neil removed the remains of a small welded patch-section from the rear inner sill. We will be carrying on with this part of the restoration in the next issue.

1971 MGB GT

Part Five:
Our 1971 MGB GT project car gets new metal welded into the rear suspension mounting, chassis member and front chassis leg. Peter Simpson explains how it's done.

OUR MGB GT project car looked in a sorry state when we left it last month. It was minus most of its floorpan and the nearside half of the central crossmember.

We had also removed all the sill structure, apart from the back half of the inner sill. This time we'll be taking off the last pieces of sill and floor and then repairing the adjacent rear spring mounting point, the rear chassis leg-to-castle section join lip, and doing localised repair work on the rear end of the front chassis leg.

On the MGB, each rear chassis leg is attached to the sills by spot welds and leg and sill meet inside the cabin just in front of the rear bulkhead. The leg runs to the back of the car, sweeping up over the axle and providing a rear spring shackle location point.

The front chassis legs, which run back along each side of the engine bay from the front of the car, are also attached to their respective sill. However, because they run parallel to each other, they can't join the sill directly. Instead, there's a central crossmember, which runs across from one side of the car to the other, linking both sills and the back of the chassis legs. This was cut in half and removed last month.

Thus the sills, central crossmember and chassis legs together form two continuous members, each running the whole length of the car.

Adjacent to the rear chassis leg-to-sill join is the forward rear spring mounting plate. The plate sits, facing upwards, between the chassis leg and bulkhead, under the floor. To strengthen this area a reinforcing plate is sandwiched between the floor and spring plate.

SPECIAL TOOLS	
■ MIG welder	■ Tape measure
■ Angle grinder	■ Electric drill
■ Hammer and cold chisel	■ Set of drill bits
■ Tin snips or similar	■ Rotary wire brush

REAR SPRING MOUNTING AND CHASSIS REPAIRS

1 There are three separate pieces of metal sandwiched together on this rear corner of the floor. Immediately under the floor there's a triangular spring mount reinforcing plate. Below that is the forward rear spring mount. The trick is to carefully remove the two upper layers without damaging the third.

2 Experts usually find it quicker to remove the remains of the floorpan and reinforcing plate together. The inexperienced should be very careful and take off one layer at a time, to avoid damaging the spring mounting plate.

3 The spring mounting plate exposed and relatively unscathed. Note the tab along the back, which is why you have to go steady; the reinforcing plate sits on top of it beneath the floorpan.

7 Remains of the inner sill can now be extracted. You may need to drive a chisel between inner sill and chassis leg. Before doing anything too drastic make certain you've dealt with all spot welds.

8 Neil went behind the rear bulkhead to remove more rust. Here he tackles the lip, which the castle section sits on. Some came away with the sill/castle; the remainder was cut back to solid metal.

9 Then Neil measured the length of metal cut away, so he could make a repair section to suit. Note the filed-away semi-circle in the new piece to match up with the old drain hole. it is easier to trim the new steel to size when fitted.

Consequently, there are three thicknesses of sheet metal in the outer rear corners of an MGB's doorpan, spot welded together to form a strong, reinforced mounting area.

CHECK YOUR LEGS

GENERALLY speaking, front chassis legs don't rust as much as rears and certainly not as readily as sills. Oil leaking out from the engine sees to that.

However, with MGBs, severe front chassis leg rust usually means the end of that particular shell's life. Although it's possible to replace a front chassis member, it's not at all easy, and a shell this bad will inevitably need extensive repairs elsewhere.

Therefore, it's usually much more cost-effective to fit a new shell if the front legs have gone. So, if you want a car to rebuild, look for one that has repairable front chassis legs.

If, on the other hand, you're after a reshell project, go for one with rotten legs, it'll be cheaper.

DOWN TO WORK

WE probed the chassis legs on our car before choosing it as a project. Although the front ends may need attention when we

repair the oil cooler panel in front of the engine, both legs appear to be repairable.

The repairs we have carried out to the rear ends are always

required when the crossmember is changed.

You will notice that some of this month's cutting is being done with an air chisel. This pro-

fessional equipment is quicker and, once you've mastered how to control the chisel, a lot easier. However, it's certainly not essential and a more DIY-friendly

4 Neil Fincham then removed the remnants of inner sill, which were still attached to the front section of the rear chassis leg. First, however, he had to remove all the paint on the chassis leg before the spot welds could be found.

5 Then Neil drilled through each spot weld in turn. A special spot weld remover makes the job easier, but isn't essential. Using a conventional drill, Neil made a small pilot hole in the centre of each weld and followed each of these up with a hole to take out the complete weld.

6 Next, he cut through the seam weld between the inner sill and the doorpost. You also have to separate the inner sill from the chassis leg inside the wheelarch, where there's usually lots of rust.

10 It's best to attach a curved repair section using a series of tack welds, starting at one end and then bending the repair section to fit as you go. Later, join the tacks with continuous weld.

11 After thoroughly cleaning the rear suspension bottom mount plate and associated tabs, Neil positioned the new reinforcement plate and seam-welded along the chassis and bulkhead edges.

12 After welding along the join with the mounting plate, 17 holes were drilled through the reinforcement plate to the mounting plate beneath.

RESTORATION PROJECT

THE MGB HIVE

This restoration is being carried out for us by Neil Fincham of the MGB Hive at Parsons Drove, near Wisbech, Cambridgeshire (01945 700500). As well as being the region's leading supplier of MGB parts, the MGB Hive also undertakes all kinds of repair and restoration work, from routine servicing upwards.

BACK ISSUES

■ Our MGB GT restoration started in the September 1994 issue. In this we introduced the car and advised on buying a suitable example for restoration.
■ October 1994 saw the car being stripped and the front wings removed.
■ In November 1994 the wipers, glasswork, lights and petrol tank came out.
■ Last month, we attacked sills, floorpan and centre crossmember with angle grinder and chisel.

Copies of all these issues are available from our Back Issues department, priced £2.50 UK, £3.50 overseas. Send your full name and address plus issue(s) required to: Practical Classics Back issues, Tower Publishing Services, Sovereign Park, Market Harborough LE16 9EF.

NEXT MONTH
FRONT BULKHEAD REPAIRS

angle grinder and cutting disc will do just as well — if slower.

I'd advise against using an air chisel to separate the three floor/spring hanger plates unless you're experienced and know exactly how to control a chisel.

As the picture sequence shows, you have to remove the top two layers, leaving the bottom one intact, and just to make matters even more complicated, there's a tab on top of the bottom plate's back, which also has to be left untouched. It's safer to use a cutting disc, or a hammer and cold chisel, and take the top surfaces away in sections.

REAR SPRING MOUNTING AND CHASSIS REPAIRS continued

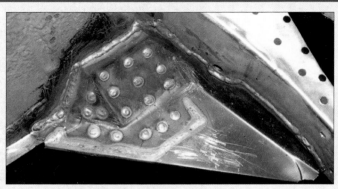

13 All the drilled holes were then plug-welded after which the welds were ground flat. Don't forget to do this, because the floorpan goes on top, and you'll find it impossible to get it to sit flat if there's a weld or two in the way.

14 Next, Neil attacked the rear of the front chassis leg where it joins the centre crossmember. Because the inner edge was sound and could be used as a reference, there was no need to waste time measuring what was being cut off.

15 Probing further up the channel revealed a few holes. A hammer and chisel can be used to remove rot, but an angle grinder and cutting disc are quicker and neater.

16 Neil made a repair section for the channel from sheet steel, to the correct width. It's over-length because the end tucks under the centre crossmember and is welded to it.

17 New section was then welded in. Note the scissor jack and wooden block supporting the chassis leg, and a further jack and block supporting the gearbox from underneath. The first one is there in case the leg needs to be moved.

18 Neil then fabricated a small repair piece for the end of the vertical section. This incorporated the two bent-up tabs, pictured in the above photograph, as used on the original. It was made to line up with the matching tab opposite.

1971 MGB GT

Part Six:
Our MGB GT project car needed repairs to the bulkhead. This can be a complicated job, but Peter Simpson shows the easy way to tackle it.

O NE job leads to another when repairing a rusty unitary construction bodyshell. That's why our 1971 MGB GT had its bulkhead repaired before fitting a new sill assembly and floorpan.

The bulkhead has to be repaired first because its lower end runs underneath and is spot-welded to the floor. It is formed from two lower panels, one each side of the transmission tunnel, and roughly the same height.

Above that there's a horizontal shelf section which the heater sits on. The outer edge of each lower panel joins the windscreen support, and there are a couple of holes so that the splash panel can be bolted on.

The inner sill ends on the bulkhead, as does the front inner

wing on the other (engine) side.

On UK specification cars the pedals and steering column poke through the offside bulkhead panel. However, the same shell was used for left and righthand-drive cars, so there are control holes on both sides. The unused ones are plugged with rubber, and the pedal hole on the horizontal section is covered by a bolt-on plate.

Replacing a complete lower bulkhead panel is a big job. First the engine and gearbox have to come out. Then you have to remove almost everything under the dash including the heater ducts. If you're doing the offside bulkhead there are the controls, including the steering column.

Then you can start cutting through the welded joints with other panels. As you can imagine this involves a lot of work.

Fortunately, there is a much easier way of tackling the job, as Neil Fincham demonstrated when I watched him at work on our car at the MGB Hive.

The technique is to cut the bulkhead just inside the inner wing joint. Removing this piece

SPECIAL TOOLS

Angle grinder
MIG welder
Hammer and cold chisel
Tin snips or similar
Self-locking wrench

BULKHEAD REPAIRS

1 First job was to unscrew and remove blanking plate on bulkhead top. Held on by crosshead screws, you won't get them out with a screwdriver. This is where the pedals are on lefthand-drive MGBs.

2 There should be a bolt-on splash panel here. However, it was long gone as were its holes in the bulkhead edge. Strip had been welded on, to stop the passenger's feet from getting wet. So off it came.

5 The trumpet bottom's usually non-existent, thanks to the combined effects of road salt and water thrown up by the wheels. But you'll still have to separate the remains of its fixing tab.

6 it's time to remove the main bulkhead section. There's a tab (which has to remain intact) running the full length of the inner wing, so cut just outside that first, not right into the corner.

is relatively straightforward, as you'll see from pictures one to six below.

Then, after cutting the new panel down to suit, it is butt-welded on to the cut-back old one. Of course, this means that the car has a welded join that wasn't on it originally. But as long as the weld is strong and continuous there's no structural reason why you shouldn't do this, and the weld can always be ground down to hide it.

The old bulkhead must be cut back until sound metal is reached, not just to the inner wing. Usually you'll stop about ½in inside the inner wing joint.

Don't use one weld to join the inner wing and the two bits of bulkhead. That's bodging, and will never be as strong as the original. However, two separate welds will be, as long as they penetrate properly.

The tricky bit is cutting the new bulkhead panel to size. The best way is to clamp the complete new panel in position over the remains of the old one from inside the car once you've finished cutting it back.

Welding in a bulkhead repair section cut from a complete panel. The section was clamped in two places. Yes, before you write in, the carburettors were drained of petrol before we started welding.

3 Next to be removed was inner wing support or trumpet. Separate the piece above the trumpet by cutting through the seam, leaving the inner wing intact. Then, cut down behind the triangular section.

4 That's because the trumpet box-section continues back. So, probably, does the rot. The entire panel may need replacing, but this section should come out first to reach the horizontal piece.

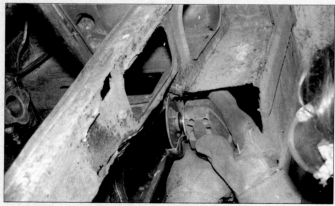

7 The join should be inside the inner wing, so Neil ground away metal behind the tab, and in until all rot was removed. This was about ½in inboard of the inner wing, an inch at the top.

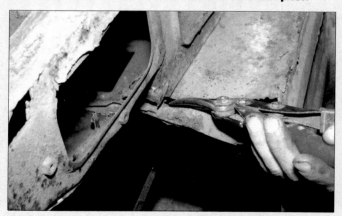

8 If the front of the inner wing box section is rotten (most are) cut it away next. It's not used as a reference for fitting the bulkhead, and access is easier with the bulkhead out of the way.

THE MGB HIVE

This restoration is being carried out for us by Neil Fincham of the MGB Hive at Parsons Drove, near Wisbech, Cambridgeshire (01945 700500).

As well as being the region's leading supplier of MGB parts, the MGB Hive also undertakes all kinds of repair and restoration work, from routine servicing upwards.

You may need to disconnect some wires and control cables. Then scribe down the edge of the cut from under the bonnet. Now you can remove the new panel and cut it.

Cut just inside the line you've marked, so the piece you're going to fit is slightly bigger than needed. Then you've got some metal left and can fine-tune the panel fit by offering it up from inside and grinding away until flush.

The bulkhead is too thick for snips and you'll certainly need an angle grinder and cutting disc. You'll also need a grinder to cut away the bulkhead inside the inner wing — there's no room for snips. You can buy good grinders for under £50.

BULKHEAD AND REPAIRS continued

9 Nearside bulkhead piece. It fits to the transmission tunnel's vertical face at the front; the bottom tucks underneath floor-pan. Holes on the left are for splash panel — missing from our car.

10 Our bulkhead needed cutting like this; fairly typical, though it varies depending how rusty it is. Don't try to get the size right first time. Better to cut slightly too big and grind down.

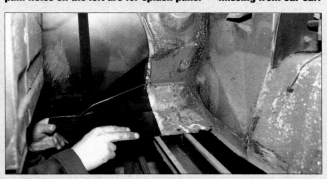

11 The section has to be positioned spot-on, but there's lots of references. The bottom tuck-under fold and double pressing at the top should form straight lines across both pieces.

12 When you're satisfied with the position, clamp the repair section to the chassis rail. Check the position again and fine-tune before fitting second welding clamp as in heading photo.

13 With repair section position fixed, Neil made first of two welds to fix it. From inside car, he butt-welded new bulkhead section to main bulkhead, making the righthand weld-line.

14 Then he welded inner wing tab to bulkhead (heading photo). Weld whole length of bulkhead down to front of chassis leg. This joint is exposed to road-dirt, so use lots of seam sealant.

1971 MGB GT

Part Seven:
Our project car gets a new inner sill, castle section and floorpan. Peter Simpson explains how it was done.

AFTER cutting out rot and strengthening vital parts of the body structure, we've made good progress fitting new panels to our MG. The passenger side now sports a new floorpan, inner sill and sill bottom or castle section.

The critical part when carrying out the work is clamping the castle section into place. It runs along the bottom of the inner sill with its outer edge exactly 5.5in from the top of the inner sill, along both panels' entire length. That sounds simple enough, but isn't particularly easy to achieve.

Neil Fincham (the MGB Hive's welder-in-chief) has devised a special tool for the job. As you can see from picture 9, it consists of a scissor jack with an old axle stand top welded to it.

Plates have been welded to the jack's base to widen it sufficiently for another jack to sit on it, and a small plate has been welded across the cup top.

Thus, if the castle section's inner edge is jacked into place, and the jack that's supporting it is sitting on the modified jack's extended base, lowering the modified jack will pull down on a pair of clamps gripping the castle section's outer edge. Hey presto — the outer edge's position can be finely adjusted at will.

Then, when the position is finally correct, the castle-section is clamped into place prior to welding.

Apart from that, the work is fairly straightforward. At least it should be, as long as you've done all the preparation work I've outlined over the past few months properly. But don't forget to remove all the primer from surfaces being joined — especially the new panels.

Despite what some people think, most panel primers are not weld-through. But you must protect the joint, otherwise it will start to rust within weeks.

SPECIAL TOOLS
- Six welding clamps
- Imperial tape-measure
- Modified scissor jack (see text)
- Unmodified scissor jack
- Welding equipment

INNER SILL, CASTLE SECTION, CENTRE CROSSMEMBER AND FLOORPAN

1 Front of the new inner sill butts on to the new bulkhead section which we saw being fitted in the last issue. The back, shown here, sits inside the rear chassis leg/corner section.

2 Inner sill's back sits up against the chassis leg and on top of the outward facing lip which runs along the chassis leg bottom. We demonstrated the repair of that chassis leg in the January 1995 issue.

5 With the back firmly clamped, Neil tack-welded the inner sill's front edge to the bulkhead. It should be positioned with the top edge up against the windscreen support/A-post section.

6 Then he welded the top seam. To replicate the original spot-welds at the rear, Neil plug-welded through numerous drilled holes in the corner section (see pictures 1 and 4) on to the inner sill.

There are two ways of protecting the joint. Either coat the surfaces to be joined with weld-through primer before you start, or cover the whole join thoroughly with seam-sealer afterwards to keep the moisture out. Of course there's nothing to stop you doing both.

As you can see from the final few pictures in the sequence, the floorpan is welded in from above and below. The front and back sit on tabs attached to the front and rear bulkhead. You can't get to these joints with welding clamps, so you may need an assistant to press down on the panel while you weld it in, to make sure that it contacts properly.

There's just one other point to note, which concerns the centre crossmember. This runs across the middle of the car, from one sill to the other, as one piece. But you can't really remove it as one piece because to do so you'll have to take out the floor of both sides, which isn't advisable as there's a good chance the shell will then distort .

The usual procedure is to cut

MGB Hive body repair specialist Neil Fincham, alongside all the new panels usually needed to restore the nearside sill and floor. The main central crossmember (on the left) was cut and replaced in two halves.

3 However, it wouldn't go right into its correct position until Neil (who should be wearing gloves) had used his hammer and chisel to cut away a few remnants of the inner wheelarch.

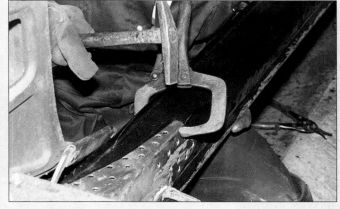

4 Next Neil clamped the sill into place. It has to be hard up against the corner section. Note that the primer has been ground away along the bottom — remove it from all surfaces to be welded.

7 It's now time to fit the new castle, or sill bottom section. This runs along the entire length of the inner sill, and is welded to its lower lip. As we'll see in a moment, its position is critical.

8 Front of the castle section goes under the bulkhead bottom edge like this, not between it and the inner sill as might seem logical. Clamp it to the outer lip to check for fit before welding.

THE MGB HIVE

This restoration is being carried out for us by Neil Fincham of the MGB Hive at Parsons Drove, near Wisbech, Cambridgeshire (01945 700500).

As well as being the region's leading supplier of MGB parts, the MGB Hive also undertakes all kinds of repair and restoration work, from routine servicing upwards.

through the middle of the old crossmember, under the transmission tunnel, and remove the nearside half only. The new crossmember is then cut to suit and welded in place. It should be tack-welded to the old offside half to ensure accurate location when that is replaced with a new section. In due course the two halves will be joined by a continuous weld. Done properly, it's as strong as the original, and a lot easier than trying to fit it as one piece.

So with the inner sill in place, are we moving on to the outer next month? I'm afraid not.

Before that can go on, the A-post/windscreen support sectio needs rebuilding. That can't be done until the inner wing top, and the windscreen surround have been repaired.

The latter includes the sectio which meets the front wing and is a very common rot-spot. So I'm afraid the outer sill will hav to gather dust in the panel store for a little while longer.

INNER SILL, CASTLE SECTION, CENTRE CROSSMEMBER AND FLOORPAN

9 To position the castle section correctly, you must support its inner edge, but still be able to move the outer up and down. Hence this ingenious modified scissor jack - see text for details.

10 Neil's jack is extremely efficient too. Using the two jacks, adjust the castle section's position until the distance between top of inner sill and bottom of castle section is exactly 5.5in.

13 Centre crossmember is usually replaced in two halves when fitted as part of a full rebuild. It lines up with the front chassis leg, inner sill and the crossmember's other half.

14 Now it's time to fit new floorpan. It mounts on an inward-facing lip, which runs along the inner sill's bottom. Form upward step along outer edge like this, so it sits flush with bottom of inner sill.

17 Next clamp floor's outer edge hard against inner sill — you'll need two long-reach welding clamps for this. Alternatively get an assistant to apply pressure on the floor when welding.

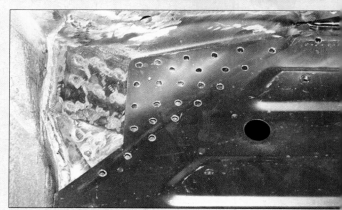

18 At the back, the drilled-out section goes directly on top of the spring reinforcing plate. If it won't sit straight make sure you've properly cleaned up the welds underneath.

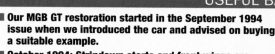

NEXT ISSUE
REPAIRING THE WINDSCREEN SURROUND

- Our MGB GT restoration started in the September 1994 issue when we introduced the car and advised on buying a suitable example.
- October 1994: Stripdown starts and front wings are removed.
- November 1994: Further stripping, including glass and fuel tank.
- December 1994: Sill, floorpan and crossmember removal.

- January 1995: Front chassis leg and underfloor rear spring mount repairs.
- February 1995: Repairs to outer edge of front bulkhead.

Copies of back issues are available from our Back Issues department, price £2.50 UK, £3.50 overseas. Send full name and address, plus details of issue(s) required to: Practical Classics Back Issues, Tower Publishing Services, Sovereign Park, Market Harborough LE16 9EF (01858 468888).

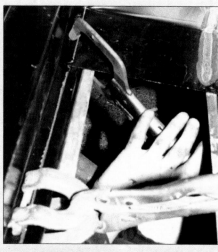

11 Now clamp the castle section firmly in position along its entire length, with clamps spaced approximately 9-10in apart. Then double-check the position of the castle section.

12 Neil then welded on the castle section. First he made tack-welds about 4in apart. Then, after checking the position yet again, he joined the tacks to form a continuous weld.

5 Neil drilled holes in all panels that will be sandwiched or sitting on top of others. These will be plug-welded. It's important that all primer is removed from surfaces to be welded.

16 As long as you've prepared it properly, the floor should now fit straight into its space. Ours almost did. We had to cut a tiny slither off the front before it would sit completely square.

9 The floorpan's welded in from on top and underneath. First Neil plug-welded through the drilled holes to secure the inner and rear spring mounting plate joints.

20 Then, from underneath, he seam-welded along the joints with the transmission tunnel, front chassis leg, central crossmember, front and rear bulkheads, and the inner sill.

1971 MGB GT

Part eight:
The windscreen support panels are being repaired before the outer sill is fitted. Peter Simpson explains the logic behind this.

FOR THIS instalment we are moving away from the sills to start work on the front scuttle and inner wing sections. If this area needs repairing, it's usually done before the outer sill goes on, as it affects the front wing's position. It's also much easier to align the sill with the wing bolted on for reference.

No factory-made panels are being used for repairs. Instead, we're restoring the existing ones using workshop-made sections cut from sheet steel.

The sections needed are quite small and also relatively easy to cut and shape, though as I've mentioned in the captions, it's often easier to cut a card template to shape first, and then trace round that on the metal.

The work itself is very straightforward and the picture and caption sequence really says it all. There are just two things that require a little extra care. First, make sure the long vertical scuttle repair section is tight against the bulkhead top all round. If it's not, the front wing won't fit properly. And don't try

to fill in the two drain holes!

The other slightly difficult pa[rt] is ace bodyman Neil Fincham's technique for forming the rear horizontal repair section. Here the difficulty is that you can't g[et] clamps in to hold the metal in place during welding. So, as you can see, Neil formed the sectio[n] oversize at the back, but with the extra metal bent slightly upwards.

While pressing down on the section to hold it in place, he welded the front edge. Then, with the front secure, he cut the back down to size and welded that. Neil used a grinder to remove the metal, but beginner[s] might find it easier to use tin-snips — at least to form the rough shape.

Next time, we'll be moving a[...]

SPECIAL TOOLS
- Aviation snips
- One pair of long reach welding clamps
- Tape measure
- Card and scissors
- Welding equipment

REPAIRING THE SCUTTLE AND INNER WINGS

1 Scuttle to front wing joint. Vertical section is double-skinned, as windscreen support panel laps over flitch panel's top. Neil ground away support panel edge, avoiding damage to flitch underneath.

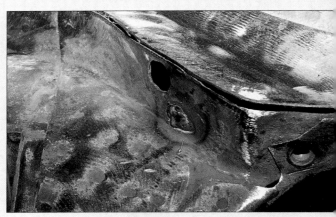

2 Bottom surface was generally sound, apart from a pinhole, which Neil welded up. Note surface corrosion though — that's what hap[pens] when water is trapped between layers of unprotected metal.

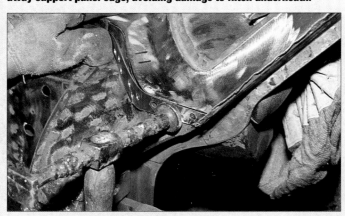

5 Next Neil tapped the rest of the section round into place, aligning the top edge exactly. Unless you're trying to create a concours job the bottom edge's shape and position isn't too critical.

6 Repair section was then plug-welded into position along its whol[e] length, starting from the front. Make sure it's sitting snugly — yo[u] can't clamp it in place. Two holes were left clear of weld.

The MGB HIVE

The project car featured on these pages belongs to and is being restored by the MGB Hive of Parsons Drove, Cambs.

The MG will be for sale when work is completed later in the year. If you are interested in buying the car, or just want to see how work is progressing, contact proprietor Nigel Petch (01945 700500). He says that readers are always welcome.

As well as being the region's leading supplier of MGB parts, the company undertakes servicing and repairs along with restoration work at their Fenland premises near Wisbech.

...le further down the front end, ...ckling a short rotten section of ...ner wing, and fitting a new ...osing panel/trumpet section ...er the top. This is a very com...only-needed repair.

For maximum life, paint any ...uble-skinned bare metal sur...ces with a weld-through primer ...fore they are hidden by repair ...ctions.

Neil Fincham, the MGB Hive's body repair specialist, welds in a new windscreen support panel edge.

Next Neil made a tapered repair section from sheet steel. He was able to cut it by eye, but those of us who are less experienced ...uld be better off using a card template to avoid possible wastage.

4 After bending section roughly to shape and drilling a series of holes down its entire length, Neil tack-welded on back edge first. Note the thick gloves — never weld without proper protection.

The reason was because they are both over the water drainage holes. Instead, Neil took them out to size using a round file. Note ...at the top joint has not been welded at this stage.

8 That's because the outer edge was rotten in two places, which had to be cut out. Aviation snips or a Monodex nibbler are ideal for this; a hammer and chisel cause too much distortion.

REPAIRING THE SCUTTLE AND INNER WINGS (CONTINUED)

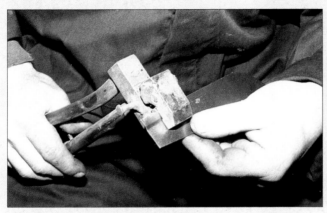

9 Again, Neil was able to cut the repair section by eye, but remember it's cheaper to throw away a miscut card template than a piece of metal. Note the joddle-joint being formed.

10 This joddled section slips underneath the cut-out surface. Then clamp it in place along the joddled edge, using a pair of long welding clamps coming in from under the bonnet opening.

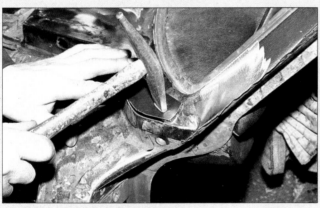

11 Back repair section had to be made differently, as it's virtually impossible to clamp. Neil's technique was to make it oversize at the back, and tap down to the correct profile.

12 Then, after welding the front edge, the back edge could be ground to shape and welded down too. If you're careful, you can do this without damaging the original metal.

13 Neil then started probing the front pillar guttering. it looked very sound — until he started poking with a sharp instrument. Check whole way up — you sometimes find rot at the top.

14 To remove the rot, Neil cut out the whole affected area. Then he welded in a replacement strip. Neat welding is required here. The bottom edge can be trimmed to size once it's fitted.

1971 MGB GT

Part nine: Peter Simpson explains what is involved in repairing the inner wing, lower windscreen support sections and bulkhead closing panel.

THE metal weevil does most damage when it can chomp away unseen, and one area that suffers badly on MGBs is the bulkhead and front wheelarch area.

In our April issue, we left the 1971 MGB GT project car with the windscreen surround and top panel repaired. Below these there is the supporting box sections and bulkhead closing panel, and these are the areas that we are concentrating on this time.

As they are closely connected to the inner wing, it's usual to repair both at the same time. There's a triangular trumpet section running outwards from the inner wing to the windscreen support area. Or rather there should be — on most cars needing restoration it's usually very corroded, and ours was no exception.

It's also normal practice when doing a full rebuild to repair this area before fitting the outer sill, because the sill and sill membrane section fit underneath a lip along the closing panel's bot-

The MGB HIVE

The project car featured on these pages belongs to and is being restored by the MGB Hive of Parsons Drove, Cambs.

The MG will be for sale when work is completed later in the year. If you are interested in buying the car, or just want to see how work is progressing, contact proprietor Nigel Petch (01945 700500). He says that readers are always welcome.

As well as being the region's leading supplier of MGB parts, the company undertakes servicing and repairs along with restoration work at their Fenland premises near Wisbech

tom edge, and you can then use the closing panel as an additional reference point.

If you make a series of drill holes through the bottom edge, you can plug-weld through to obtain a clean, neat joint. In fact carefully made plug-welds here can look exactly like factory spot welds.

Inner wing rot on the project

REPAIRING THE SCUTTLE AND INNER WINGS

1 This section of inner wing would be covered by the trumpet section, but ours had rusted away. Neil is using an air chisel. A hammer and cold chisel will do the job as well, but a lot slower.

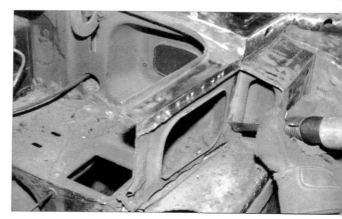

2 Rear section of front inner wing is tackled next. Seams are split by cutting between two layers of metal to separate spot-welds. Another way is to cut clear of seam and remove the tabs afterwards.

5 Heater support panel repair section was made up from sheet steel by Neil. Note the stepped-down joddle section which runs under the existing metal, and the flange at the other side.

6 Rear inner wing repair section goes in next. Drill a series of holes in the bottom tab of the repair section, then plug-weld through these and the holes in inner wing top edge to secure panel.

MGB Hive body repair specialist Neil Fincham welds in the inner wing repair section after trimming it to fit.

...ar is fairly typical of what you ...nd on most Bs — the area ...ehind the trumpet and box-sec...ons are usually the worst. ...ometimes you find more exten...ve rust down the outer wing ...int lip, and occasionally there ...ill be holes behind the shock absorbers. Even so, it's invariably easier to repair the existing panel than fit a complete new inner wing .

The only other point to note is that the nearside inner wing has the bonnet stay pivot attached. This isn't on the repair section, so has to be transferred —drill through the spot welds holding it on — or maybe you will only need pliers to pull it off.

Finally, a reminder that working on cars can be dangerous. Remember eyesight cannot always be restored!

SPECIAL TOOLS
- Tinsnips
- Hammer and cold chisel
- Powered cutting equipment
- Welding kit
- Metal scriber

3 Now heater support panel outer edge can be removed by cutting through spot welds. Inner cut line should be directly under where the inner wing sits — unless there's rot further inboard.

4 Then clean up and straighten all the tab surfaces etc, to leave free of rust and paint for welding. Fortunately, the back of our inner wing top and outer wing mating surface was sound.

7 Cut front repair section to size. It fits on top of, not behind, the raised tab running down rear section's front edge. Sections are supplied oversize at the top to allow for trimming.

8 Front repair section also includes part of inward-facing wheelarch area. Clamp it into place over the existing lower inner wing, make scribe mark and then cut to suit.

REPAIRING INNER WINGS (CONTINUED)

NEXT ISSUE ••••••• FITTING AN OUTER SILL

9 Section is then tack-welded into place. Welds are then joined into a continuous bead along the bottom. Finally, the lower joint is ground smooth to make it virtually invisible.

10 Top repair section comes as full length and has to be trimmed to size. Make sure the section you've cut out covers all the rot, as it·can be extensive. Then weld in new section.

11 Welded joints are then covered with seam sealer to keep out moisture, and all the repair sections painted. The MGB Hive make extensive use of Hammerite to protect repaired areas.

12 Now we tackle the bulkhead closing panel. This is removed in four sections to preserve original joining tabs. After removing rust to reveal spot welds, Neil cut this bit out.

13 Large bottom section is removed in one piece. Most of this had been freed during sill, bulkhead and heater support panel work. Gloves are essential when handling rusty metal.

14 Finally, Neil cuts out door hinge supporting section. Because of limited access, tinsnips are being used. The remaining metal on top of the retaining tabs was then ground away.

15 Lining-up the new closing panel, using splash panel bolts to hold it in place. Remove paint along tab lines inside, then weld along them to secure panel; seam-seal afterwards.

16 Last new panel to fit is the replacement trumpet section. Paint inside before sliding it into place. You may need to open up the slots along its outer edge to fit the trumpet inside.

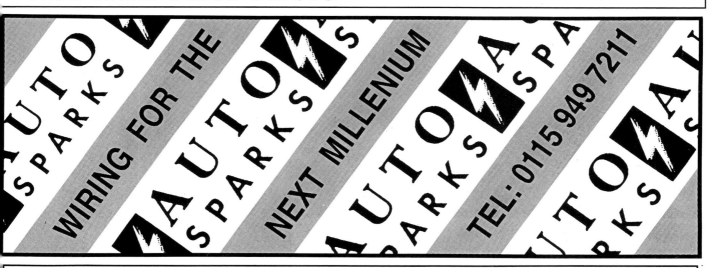

MGB GT

Part ten: Peter Simpson explains how new centre and outer sills were fitted to our 1971 MGB GT project car.

The MGB HIVE

The project car featured on these pages belongs to and is being restored by the MGB Hive of Parsons Drove, Cambs.

The MG will be for sale when work is completed later in the year. If you are interested in buying the car, or just want to see how work is progressing, contact proprietor Nigel Petch (01945 700500). He says that readers are always welcome.

As well as being the region's leading supplier of MGB parts, the company undertakes servicing and repairs along with restoration work at their Fenland premises near Wisbech.

AT LONG last we have fitted the first new outer panel to our project MGB GT. The panel in question is the outer sill, which will probably be inspected closely by potential purchasers and MoT testers in years to come. Conversely, most of the metal previously replaced during the rebuild has been of structural underpinnings and won't be seen when the car's complete.

Each MGB sill structure consists of four basic members, which make up double box sections flattened to form wedge-shape sections at each end.

Fitting the new inner sill and castle section

were covered in the December issue, then work in the bulkhead area had to be tackled before we could go back and complete the job by fitting the centre and outer sill panels.

The hardest part of the whole outer sill fitting process is lining the sill up correctly. As the pictures show, the door has to be refitted first. Make sure it's aligned properly with the rear wing. You also have to temporarily refit the front wing and align the door to that, too. Our restorer Neil Fincham didn't need to do this as he's done enough MGBs to be able to judge the door's correct position.

The wing then has to come off again before

the outer sill is fitted; this is because the side front end tucks underneath it. If necessary the wing can go back on again afterwards as an extra guide to sill alignment.

As you've probably gathered, this stage of the rebuild can take several hours but it pays to take your time and do it properly. Virtually every other panel gap on that side depends on the sill's position being right, so the sill will have a big effect on the finished car's appearance.

When welding one flat surface on top of another, it's a good idea to coat the surfaces being joined with weld-through primer first.

FITTING THE CENTRE AND OUTER SILL PANELS

1 Neil started by drilling a row of 5mm holes along the centre sill's lower edge, where it will butt to the castle section. If you're unsure where to drill, clamp the panel in place, scribe a line along the castle section bottom, and drill just inboard of it.

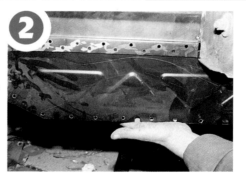

2 Next, after cleaning off round drill holes on castle section outer edge, centre sill section was pushed into place. Note that it tucks underneath bulkhead like this. This edge must not be welded yet, as the outer sill also has to tuck underneath.

3 After clamping centre sill in place (you'll need least seven pairs of welding clamps to secure it Neil made two tack-welds along top edge, without touching outward-facing surface. Then drilled holes were plug-welded to secure bottom edge

7 Before fitting outer sill, Neil drilled holes 3cm apart along outer sill bottom edge. He ground away primer around holes, so weld could spread underneath. Inside of the sill was painted with Hammerite, keeping clear of surfaces to be welded.

8 Offering up the sill. Push the panel up into place, making sure the gap between door and sill is even. You might find that the door needs pulling in or out slightly. Temporarily refitting the front wing will give you another reference.

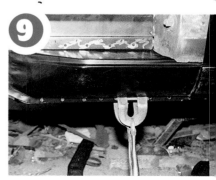

9 Don't forget that the front section goes up behind the bulkhead. You will need four pairs of welding clamps along the bottom edge, and a further two or three along the top. Make sure B-post bottom tabs (right of picture) are rust-free underneath

Moment of truth. Neil Fincham of the MGB Hive lines up the new nearside outer sill.

▶ECIAL TOOLS

- At least seven pairs of welding clamps
- Electric drill and 5mm bit
- Angle grinder, safety gloves, goggles
- MIG welder

▶e recommended this before in this series, ⬛ a few readers have been in touch via the *⬛actical Classics* Helpline, asking where ⬛s can be obtained.

Some accessory shops may sell it, and it is available under various trade names from motor and paint factors. Look in your Yellow Pages for details of one close to you. It's expensive stuff, so use it only on surfaces you are going to weld through, not as a general primer.

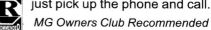

NEXT ISSUE:
Oil cooler panel replacement

4 ▶e plug-welds were then ground smooth. This is ⬛ortant, otherwise the outer sill won't sit ⬛aight. Grinding along whole edge also gives a ⬛an surface on to which to attach the outer sill. ⬛ety gloves and eye protection are important.

5 Inner-facing surface of centre sill was coated with Hammerite before fixing. Neil tackled the outer surface next. Bottom edge was left clear; you can't weld through Hammerite. However, special weld-through primers are available for areas like this.

6 To get the outer sill in the correct position, the door has to be fitted. Align the door's top edge with the top of the rear wing, and check that the swage line is level. Ensure there is an even gap between door and wing from top to bottom.

0 ⬛ edge was secured first by a series of short ⬛m welds along the top. Don't worry if the top ⬛ges aren't even — they can be ground straight ⬛r; as long as you carried out stage eight prop-⬛y, the sill will be positioned correctly.

11 As you can see, Neil has a rather primitive, but effective way of pressing the outer sill right up into place. He then plug-welded through the drilled holes. Do this neatly, and your plug-welding will look just like the factory's spot-welds.

12 Series of spot-welds used to finally secure top edge. Exactly the same technique as was used at Abingdon when the car was built 25 years ago. If you don't have a spot-welder achieve same appearance by drilling through and plug-welding.

MGB GT

Part eleven: our MGB project continues as a new oil cooler panel is slotted into place. Peter Simpson reports.

The **MGB HIVE**

THE project car featured on these pages belongs to and is being restored by the MGB Hive of Parsons Drove, Cambs.

The MG will be for sale when completed. If you are interested in buying the car, or just want to see how work is progressing, contact proprietor Nigel Petch (01945 700500). *Practical Classics* readers are always welcome.

As well as being the region's leading supplier of MGB parts, the company also undertakes servicing and repairs along with restoration work at their Fenland premises near Wisbech.

WITH our 1971 MGB's sill structure finally finished, attention turned to the front end. There we came across another common problem — corrosion of the oil cooler tray.

Sitting between the radiator and the front of the car, this large flat panel helps channel air from the radiator grille through to the radiator. On an MGB it also carries the oil cooler radiator.

This panel is particularly prone to rusting around the outer edges and along the front where moisture and salt get trapped. The front edge is also prone to accident-impact damage. You can patch-repair it, but only in ways that are obvious as soon as the bonnet

is opened, so the whole panel is usually replaced during a full restoration.

However, replacing the panel isn't particularly easy as it rests on the front chassis legs and front crossmember. It's attached to these by spot-welds through to horizontal tabs running along both sides of all three members, and forms the top of these box-sections.

The tabs have to stay in place, in order that the new panel can be welded to them. But there isn't room underneath to work with a chisel and cut through between the tab and panel to separate the spot welds.

Progress can only be made by cutting out the panel in sections, as shown in the

picture sequence. Have a good look underneath before you start, so you can see exactly where the tabs are. Use this information, plus the line of indentations from the factory spot-welds, to tell you exactly where to cut, and allow an extra 5mm from the tabs in case you've made a mistake.

Then, when the main parts of the panel are out, you can tackle the strips remaining on top of the tabs separately, and at the same time clean and dress the tabs.

Occasionally, removing the cooler panel reveals serious rot in chassis legs that look rock-solid from underneath. That's because like all box-sections, chassis legs rot from

FITTING A NEW OIL COOLER TRAY

Drain radiator and disconnect hoses. Undo bolts securing radiator support panel to each inner wing and take out bolts holding oil cooler assembly. There's no need to undo the cooler pipes.

You can then lift the radiator, support panel and oil cooler assembly out of the way. Place a piece of thick corrugated card on top of the engine, and lay the radiator on that to protect it.

Next unclip the bonnet release cable and wiring loom section that runs underneath the bonnet slam panel. Our car will be rewired, so Neil just ground through the clips.

Then Neil cut along the outer edge of the main chassis leg, just outside the tab line. It's feasible to do all this with a hammer and cold chisel, but a powered chisel's much quicker.

Next he tackled the section above the chassis leg in exactly the same way. There's a short, rear-facing tab on the back of the cooler tray — leave that attached for now.

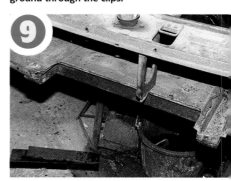

Then cut through and remove the front section o the tray. The spot welds and tabs method of holding the tray down is now very obvious. Cut round the central support strut.

MGB Hive's Neil Fincham prepares the front chassis legs and crossmember to receive their new oil cooler tray. Note the safety precautions when grinding.

...e inside out, so you don't see it until it ...reaks through. Since the whole front ...uspension is bolted on the front chassis ...gs, I strongly recommend some thorough ...robing of any suspect areas.

If you do manage to poke right through, ...'s usually easier to repair before the new ...ooler panel's fitted. Pin-holes can ...ometimes be repaired by simply plugging ...ith weld, but before doing so make sure ▶

SPECIAL TOOLS

- Angle grinder
- Welding equipment
- Rotary wire brush
- Hammer and cold chisel or powered chisel
- Molegrips and welding clamps

4

...uter edge of oil cooler tray is attached to inner ...ving by spot-welds through an upward facing tab ...n the inside edge. To locate these, Neil first ...round away the rust and undersealant.

5

Then he dealt with the spot-welds by drilling through the middle. Neil is pictured using a conventional drill bit, but a proper spot-weld cutter is quicker and makes a cleaner cut.

6

Time to attack the tray itself. Cut along the corner like this. It's far easier than trying to cut down between tab and wing, and the tab will probably be damaged or come off.

10

...fter cutting away the opposite side's outer edge, ...he rear piece was removed, again by cutting ...long outside the tab line. That surface rust in the ...ffside chassis leg needs treating.

11

Last bit. Neil removed the piece above the front crossmember by cutting along inside the tabs. Again, strips where the oil cooler tray was actually welded on remained.

12

But they didn't survive long. Neil cut or ground them away, leaving the chassis member tabs intact. He then ground these back to bright metal in preparation for welding.

all the surrounding metal is solid. If it isn't, cut back until it is. Finish off by rustproofing internal sections thoroughly with an anti-rust wax.

We fitted the new cooler panel by drilling through and then plug-welding. To spot-weld it as original, we would have needed a spot welder with arms 3ft long. Drilling and plug welding is a realistic and perfectly acceptable substitute — especially as well-made plug welds are virtually indistinguishable from factory spot-welds once painted.

We are now slightly over half-way through this series so let's look at what's still to come. Next we'll move to the back end and look at rear wing removal, followed by necessary repairs to the rear spring mounts, fitting a new boot floor and repair or replacement of the rear panel and valance.

Then, after the new rear wing's been fitted, we'll be taking a break from bodywork and move into the MGB Hive's mechanical overhaul shop, and cover the engine, gearbox and front suspension rebuild. Then it will be time to go back to the bodyshop for painting, interior trimming and final fitting-up.

NEXT ISSUE:
Rear wing removal

FITTING A NEW OIL COOLER TRAY (continued)

Exposed inner surfaces were painted to resist further corrosion. The MGB Hive use Hammerite, which can be painted directly onto light surface rust. Don't paint the surfaces to be welded.

First trial-fitting of the new panel. Neil made s▮ that all the tabs were clean and straight, and th▮ pushed the panel in and clamped it down on to the chassis legs.

Back end tabs were clamped to the rear chassis leg tabs like this. Then, from underneath, Neil scribed along all the visible tab lines. After this he unclamped and removed the panel.

Neil drilled lines of 5mm holes along all surface▮ to be joined, then welded panel in place. Tackl▮ front crossmember edge first, then the rear, in▮ then outer leg joints and finally inner wing sear▮

MGB GT

Part twelve: Peter Simpson explains how to repair a rotten MGB spring hanger and remove a rusty rear wing.

The MGB HIVE

The project car featured on these pages belongs to and is being restored by the MGB Hive of Parsons Drove, Cambs.

The MG will be for sale when work is completed later in the year. If you are interested in buying the car, or just want to see how work is progressing, contact proprietor Nigel Petch (01945 700500). He says that readers are always welcome.

As well as being the region's leading supplier of MGB parts, the company undertakes servicing and repairs along with restoration work at their Fenland premises near Wisbech.

CORROSION galore faced us when we began to tackle the rear of the body on our MGB GT project car.

Our first task was removing a rear wing and associated metalwork. This will always need repair, or complete replacement, during a restoration.

As we saw back in the March issue, the rear end of the sill structure runs behind the rear wing's front bottom edge, so to do a proper sill job, this piece of wing has to be cut away. Not really a problem — if the sill's gone this section of wing almost certainly will have too.

There's also a good chance the arch section and rear lower corner will have rotted out. The arch is prone to collecting dirt around the inner lip, and to add to the potential for trouble, there's a welded seam joint between the wing's arch section and the outer piece of the arch itself.

Once damp and dirt get into here, it's only a matter of time before serious rusting starts. If you have an MGB, and would rather not rebuild it, clean inside the wheelarches regularly and treat rust before it gets a hold.

If anything, the rear corner of the arch is even more rot-prone. Because it is in the firing line of muck thrown up by the rear wheels, it gets sprayed in dirt every time the car is used.

Corrosion can also attack the bottom of the arch from the other side, as there is a pocket between the arch and boot floor where dirt can lodge.

When faced with rot in the rear wheelarch area, you can either replace the whole wing (which is quite a major job on GTs) or change just the section below the central swage line if everything above is okay.

On Roadsters, the wing to body seam runs the length of the wing. If the factory seal fails, water will get down between the two pieces, and cause rot. As this will start at the bottom of the seam, it won't be visible until it emerges at the top.

This means that if there's any rust visible around the top of the joint, there will be

REMOVING REAR WING, OUTER ARCH AND REAR CHASSIS LEG

1 Start removing rear wing by cutting along top edge, just in front of the window rubber retaining lip. Use a hammer and cold chisel or air-chisel. Either way the metal should slice relatively easily.

2 Next cut down the front edge, just behind the front wrap-over seam. Don't worry about leaving that attached, it can be dealt with more easily later on, when the main wing is out of the way.

3 Bottom edges might not need much cutting (rust will have done most of the hard work) but if not, here's what you do. Position of arch cut isn't critical, as inner arch will be replaced anyway.

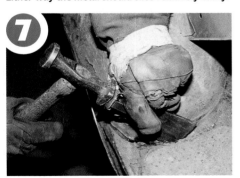

7 Now it's time to tackle rear wing closing panels, which always need replacing when a wing is repaired or changed. Cut around back of arch section, then split seam with the rear chassis leg.

8 With closing panels removed, you're usually left with a view of lots more rust. That rotten suspension mount accounts for 25 per cent of the rear suspension's security, which is rather worrying!

9 Time for a rest now and an easy job — removing this fibre closing board. Just drill out the four rivets and pull it away. But there's more rust in the open box-section beyond — what a surprise.

Neil Fincham of the MGB Hive does some final tidying-up around the rear corner and wheelarch prior to fitting a replacement rear chassis leg/spring mount section, work we'll be covering in the August issue.

serious problems further down. Bear in mind that the wing mounting lip on the bodyshell will almost certainly need attention too.

GTs, however, don't have this full-length seam, as most of the wing is underneath the rear window and attached by a join that's visible only with the window and rubber out.

The GT replacement wing panel also includes most of the rear pillar. The usual ▶

SPECIAL TOOLS

- Angle grinder and chisel (or air chisel)
- Welder (MIG or gas)
- Scissor jack and axle stands
- Hacksaw and tinsnips
- Drill plus bits, or spot-weld remover

4 Now attack top rear pillar section. Go up the back until you are above all rust in guttering (check carefully), and then cut across and down inside edge, leaving remaining gutter section intact.

5 Back corner is cut between tailgate and reversing light apertures. If the wing is bad enough to need replacing, there is not usually much holding the bottom edge to the rear valance assembly.

6 Heave ho, away we go! Once all the cuts meet, wing should be free to come off. There will be sharp, rusty edges all over it, so thick gloves are essential. Metal splinters in fingers ain't nice.

10 Chances are the wing needed replacement because of wheelarch rot, in which case outer section of the wheelarch itself will need changing too. Remove by splitting down this central seam.

11 As I mentioned earlier, cutting through MGB rear valances rarely takes much effort — most tend to be a mixture of rust and glassfibre. But remove it anyway so you have more room to work.

12 Remove the inner reinforcing section. First locate where the spot welds are at either end by wire-brushing the paint away. Then drill right through them to separate the top end fixings.

repair method here is to cut up the pillar until you reach sound metal and then trim the replacement panel to fit. The usual rot spot is along the front, where water gathers in the guttering.

In practice, fitting a bottom-half wing section is usually a satisfactory medium-term repair on a GT as long as the remainder of the wing and guttering above are, as far as you can see, totally sound.

On a Roadster, I'd normally go for a full rear wing replacement if I wanted a perfect job at the end. That's not just because the full length seam is rust-prone, but also because fitting a complete wing is not much more difficult than changing the bottom half.

Whichever method you choose, you will have to do some localised repair work on the wheelarch's outer edge at the very least, and if this needs more than a couple of medium-sized repair sections it's easier to fit a complete new section. Expect also to repair the rear lower corner.

On our car there was no question about it — the gutter was rotten almost up to the roof, so the complete wing had to come off.

Those of you who restored an MGB a few years ago might be surprised to see that we left the forward-facing post section, which carries the lock, *in situ*. That's because although replacement wings used to come complete with this piece, they no longer do.

We're also starting work on another common MGB problem area this time, the rear chassis/spring mounting area. This can be done without disturbing the rear wing (although you'll still have to remove the boot floor and closing sections), but the job is a lot easier with the wing out of the way.

As you can see, we're replacing only part of the chassis. This is easier than doing the whole lot, but it's vital that the repair section lines up correctly. I'll show you the rest of the procedure next time.

> **NEXT ISSUE**
> Fitting new rear spring hanger

REMOVING REAR WING, OUTER ARCH AND REAR CHASSIS LEG

Slice through welded seam at the bottom, working up from inside car, and pull complete section away. As you can see, ours has already had some rudimentary repairs to the nearside rear corner.

Now it's time to attack the boot floor. This is basically one panel and has to be replaced as such, but it's easiest to take it out in sections. Start by splitting it away from chassis leg inner surface.

Then cut around the three other edges to form a rectangular section like this, and lift it out carefully. Cutting away this section gives you room to work on the chassis leg and spring hanger.

Trim carefully around the back of the chassis leg, removing all remnants of attaching tabs etc, but leaving a strip of metal along valance's top edge. This must be solid enough to take tack-welds.

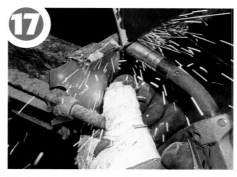

That's because next stage is to weld a small plate to the valance edge. It must have a semi-circular cut-out exactly the same size as bumper bracket. However, it mustn't be attached to chassis.

We can now start some honest probing of the leg's condition, which can only be done properly if you can see inside it. So cut away box closing section like this, so you can inspect it properly.

Ours was so bad the whole rear chassis section needed replacing. If you're crafty, you can do this without changing whole chassis leg. First unbolt back spring shackle, then jack spring away.

Then cut through leg until you reach solid metal (ie so all rot is behind the saw). That will usually be about here. Remember to salvage old bumper irons, because they're not available new.

Final job this time is to clean up all the cut edges. This involves cutting/grinding away any remaining portions of panels which have been removed, then dressing the tabs to receive the new panels.

MGB GT

WORKSHOP RATING

TIME REQUIRED 1-2 DAYS

C C C C C

Part thirteen: rear chassis repairs and boot floor replacement.
Peter Simpson is the man with the knowhow.

The MGB HIVE

The project car featured on these pages belongs to and is being restored by the MGB Hive of Parsons Drove, Cambs.

The MG will be for sale when work is completed later in the year. If you are interested in buying the car, or just want to see how work is progressing, contact proprietor Nigel Petch (01945 700500). He says that readers are always welcome.

As well as being the region's leading supplier of MGB parts, the company undertakes servicing and repairs along with restoration work at their Fenland premises near Wisbech.

OUR 1971 MGB project car was looking a little sorry for itself after removing rotten metal at the rear end. The car was minus its nearside rear wing, and the rearmost foot of the nearside chassis leg had been sawn off by the MGB Hive's body repair specialist Neil Fincham.

Tasks being tackled this time include replacing that missing piece of chassis leg and fitting the new boot floor. Since the leg runs to the back of the car from the inner sill just inside the passenger compartment, replacing the whole leg isn't a practical proposition. It's also unnecessary as it's usually the rear end that rots.

A Steelcraft repair section is available for the back end, and that's what we're using here. The usual fitting technique is to cut the leg off as far back as is necessary to remove all the rot. Then the repair section is cut to size, using the piece you've just sawn off as a reference.

You could just cut the car's leg back to suit the complete repair section. This involves one less cut, but the join will be close to the wheelarch where access is much more awkward. It's also harder to align the new piece properly with the join this far back.

Before removing the rusty leg section Neil attached a small piece of sheet steel to the remains of the rear valance. This sheet had a C-shaped cut-out which went around the rear bumper mount. That C-shaped cut-out is the positional reference. The idea is that you fit the new leg, complete with bumper iron, so that the iron is in exactly the same place as when it was attached to the original chassis.

This sounds simple enough, but don't forget that it can be out in any of three directions. As 25 per cent of the rear suspension attaches to the bit you're replacing, proper alignment of the new piece is vital.

Therefore, make the cut-out as close as possible to the bumper iron's size and attach it with an even gap top and bottom, but with the inside edge actually touching.

As we're making a welded joint where there wasn't one originally, a reinforcing

REMOVING REAR WING, OUTER ARCH AND REAR CHASSIS LEG

1 Start by cleaning off the old chassis leg's stub. Grind the edges clean. Sometimes small holes will appear, but these can be filled by plug-welding. Then face it up with a hammer and dolly like this.

2 Here's why you need that plate we tack-welded on. Neil cut the repair section to size and bolted the bumper iron to it. Then he trial fitted it so the bumper iron poked through as it had originally.

6 Then attach chassis section and weld round outside. It's best to do top first and fine-tune alignment. Note 2-3mm gap between two pieces for weld to flow in so it can be ground flat afterwards.

7 Grinding welds flat is the next stage after all three outer edges, and the reinforcement plate back edge have been welded. Some small holes may appear while you're doing this.

8 Next stage is to paint inside of chassis leg with rustproofer, then fit new closing plate. This is same length as replacement chassis leg section before trimming. Secure plate with clamps.

Neil Fincham welds on the rear chassis leg closing plate. Note the piece of metal with the semi-circular cut-out used as a reference point for positioning the new leg section.

...rip is needed behind the joint. As well as ...king the joint stronger, you can then make ...nvisible by leaving a small gap (2-3mm and ...cked by the reinforcing strip) between the ...l leg and repair section.

The weld will flow into this and once it's ...ound off and the surface primed and paint-..., the join will be flush. Take trouble here if ...u're after a perfect finish, as the chassis ▶

SPECIAL TOOLS

- Angle grinder and chisel (or air chisel)
- Welder (MIG or gas)
- Scissor jack and axle stands
- Hacksaw and tinsnips
- Drill plus bits, or spot-weld remover

...w chassis section is attached using an internal ...nforcing section. A straight butt-weld alone ...y not be strong enough. Attach this to car first, ...n it's easier to fine-tune the leg's alignment.

Welding the reinforcing section into place. Tack-weld first, then join them up by a line of continuous weld round inner edge. The three pieces of metal must be as strong as the original.

Close-up of the alignment checking piece. Get the bumper iron into exactly the same position as before the leg was chopped off. Don't forget that it can be out in any (or all) of three directions.

...tproof inner surface of closing panel, then ...k-weld into place top and bottom; push inner ...l into wheelarch edge with hammer and chisel. ...ld panel and around spring hanger holes.

Next Neil reconnected the spring hanger. Press in four new rubber bushes (two on spring, two on chassis) and then tap shackle bolt through and bolt the other side on. Bumper iron was refitted at this stage.

leg's inner edges can be seen when the boot's false floor is lifted.

Make no mistake about it, a strong weld is vital on the chassis leg. You must use continuous welds all round, including both edges of the inner reinforcing plate. Tack welds alone are not sufficient.

Our other big task this time is fitting the new boot floor and associated corner sections. The main boot floor section runs between the two chassis leg inner edges, so the offside chassis leg had to be repaired first. Both sides were remarkably similar in terms of rot and the offside needed almost exactly the same repairs as the nearside.

Once an MGB has been stripped out as comprehensively as ours, complete boot floor replacement is quite easy. The job can also be done in isolation, and the floor is often changed along with the rear panel. To do this you have to remove all the back end interior trim and seats and drop the fuel tank. It isn't necessary to remove the false floor supports, there's just about sufficient room to do it with them in place.

Removal of the floor is straightforward — you will already have chopped out the floor's sides to reach the chassis legs. The rest comes out in two pieces as shown in the pictures. Save the small reinforcing plate though (picture 13), as you can't get a replacement.

Fitting the new panel is also simple enough. Use the remains of the spot-weld on the rear panel to align the back; the fr just sits on the panel in front of it. The fr corners will probably need tapping down

Originally the boot floor was spot-weld in. Unfortunately you can't repeat this, unless your spot welder has very long ar to reach both sides of the joint. However plug welding is simple enough and a line painted plug welds is almost indistinguis able from a line of painted spot-welds.

NEXT ISSUE
Fitting a new back panel

REMOVING REAR WING, OUTER ARCH AND REAR CHASSIS LEG

Boot floor corner section is quite easy to fit. Just clamp it so the upper edges are flush like this, and weld along the top. The wheelarch joint was left unwelded to permit further work later.

When chassis legs are repaired, replace rest of boot floor. Extract old one in two pieces. Main lower section is released by cutting front and back edges. Leave spot welds visible on rear valance.

Reinforcing plate is in way of stepped section remove, first locate spot-welds, then drill thr them using either a spot-weld remover or a p drill followed by one slightly bigger than wel

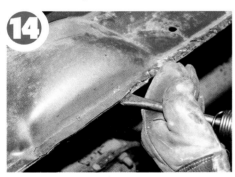

This is area immediately below reinforcing strut. Cut down front edge to remove vertical section of boot floor. Then remove tab section like this, taking care not to damage horizontal panel below it.

Neil cleaned up flanges in prepara for putting in new boot floor in. Note essential ear and e safety precautions doing work of this kind, especially im tant when working confined spaces.

Complete boot floor panel — yours for £39.95 from the **MGB Hive**. The front edge (furthest from camera) sits on horizontal surface we saw being cleaned in picture 14. Trial-fit it in position first.

Adjustment is sometimes needed to sides which butt against the chassis legs. Then drill 5mm holes about 20mm apart along all joining surfaces. Remove paint around holes so weld can flow.

Putting floor in. Front lip sits over squab/supp panel, back end is aligned with remains of sp welds, but don't weld it here if you're going change rear panel. Plug-weld other three ed

MGB GT

WORKSHOP RATING
TIME REQUIRED
1-2 DAYS
C C C C C

Part fourteen: our project car's body restoration is nearly finished. Peter Simpson tells how to replace the false boot, floor supports, rear panel and tailgate.

The MGB HIVE

The project car featured on these pages belongs to and is being restored by the MGB Hive of Parsons Drove, Cambs.

The MG will be for sale when work is completed later in the year. If you are interested in buying the car, or just want to see how work is progressing, contact proprietor Nigel Petch (01945 700500). He says that readers are always welcome.

As well as being the region's leading supplier of MGB parts, the company undertakes servicing and repairs along with restoration work at their Fenland premises near Wisbech.

AT LAST, we're starting to see real progress on our MGB GT. With completion of the rear spring hanger repair in the August issue instalment, almost all of the structural underbody work has now been finished.

From this point on, most work on the body will involve fitting outer panels. This time it's the rear panel, accompanied by the first fitting of the replacement tailgate.

Before tackling these, however, we fitted the false floor support panels, which go above the rear chassis legs in the spare wheel compartment.

Like many other sections of the car, the original rear panel was very badly corroded, particularly along the bottom edge. In fact the lower half of the panel consisted of little more than rust and filler. This is quite common on older MGB GTs, which makes it very easy to chop out.

The tailgate needed replacing due to severe corrosion along its bottom edge. Since the frame is badly affected as well as the outer skin, repair isn't viable. One solution would have been to fit a new one. But they cost £130 and, more to the point, at the time we were doing this part of the project they were temporarily unavailable.

Apart from the cost, we reckoned it would make more interesting and useful coverage if we got hold of a better secondhand tailgate and showed how to repair and fit that.

The fitting part is covered this time, and repairs will be dealt with in a later issue once we've finally stitched up the back end.

Among the MGB Hive's extensive range of cars for breaking at their Parsons Drove, Cambs premises was a 1972 example with front-end damage. Fortunately, the tailgate was in good order, apart from the glass being scratched beyond redemption. So we requisitioned that one and will fit it with the glass from our car.

Since the tailgate is aligned with the back

FITTING A NEW REAR PANEL

1 Nearside false floor and spare wheel cover support clamped in place. Rear edge sits under panel lip and when both supports are fitted they can be used as additional reference points for rear panel.

2 Clamp both supports on before welding either. It's important that they're right distance apart — if they aren't, false floor won't sit properly. Clip holes inside edges must be exactly 35½in apart.

3 Front edge sits on top of chassis leg and adjacent to side-to-side support member as shown. Clean underneath, continuous-weld around all sides and then grind welds flat so false floor sits properly.

7 Replacement rear panel was fitted temporarily and held by self-tapping screws. It won't be welded permanently until rear wings have been fitted. Bumper irons are extra alignment guides.

8 Fitting panels like this requires several clamps. Here one pair is holding flat section to chassis leg, and one is holding panel on to false floor support. Two more clamps were needed on offside of car.

9 When all four clamps were in place Neil checked floor support members' position again; attaching rear panel can move them slightly. He had to tweak out the offside member by about ⅛in.

The MGB Hive's body specialist Neil Fincham welds in a new false floor support panel.

USEFUL BACK ISSUES

● Our MGB GT restoration started in the September 1994 issue when we introduced the car and advised on buying one.

● October 1994: stripdown starts and front wings are removed.

● November 1994: further stripping, including glass and fuel tank.

● December 1994: sill, floorpan and cross-member removal.

● January 1995: front chassis leg and under-floor rear spring mount repairs.

● February 1995: repairs to outer edge of front bulkhead.

● March 1995: fitting new inner sill, castle section, crossmember and floorpan.

● April 1995: scuttle and windscreen support panel repairs.

● Spring 1995: inner wing, lower windscreen support sections and bulkhead closing panel.

● May 1995: fitting new centre and outer sills.

● June 1995: fitting a new oil cooler panel.

● July 1995: spring hanger repairs.

● August 1995: chassis leg repairs and boot floor removal.

Copies of these magazines are available from our Back Issues dept, details on page 19.

panel, it's unwise to take the tailgate and back panel off at the same time, otherwise you will lose your reference points for both.

As the back panel was to be removed, our long-suffering bodywork guru Neil Fincham reinstalled the car's original tailgate to verify that it fitted correctly. As manufacturing tolerances can vary, Neil then fitted the ▶

TOOLS REQUIRED

● Drill plus 2mm bit and angle grinder
● Hacksaw, steel ruler, hammer, cold chisel
● Four pairs of welding clamps
● Welder (MIG or gas)

---

④

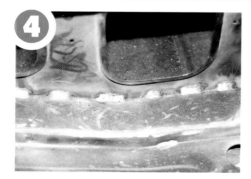

Neil attached main central part with a series of short seam-welds — this technique is acceptable as this panel isn't structural. Afterwards run seam-sealer into edge; this keeps out moisture.

⑤

Before removing the old rear panel Neil checked position of closed tailgate in relation to it. Our tailgate is past economic restoration anyway and is being replaced with a better secondhand one.

⑥

As rear panel's lower section fell apart when boot floor was replaced, removing remainder involved cutting through the gutter channelling just above where we'd previously taken off the rear wing.

⑩

Then Neil checked that the rear panel was not sitting proud or inboard of the tailgate's bottom edge. He also made sure the gap was even, taking into consideration rust along the bottom edge.

⑪

Some replacement rear panels have too much curvature in them. Result: good fit in the middle but not at the edges. Some carefully placed hammer and chisel blows may be all that's needed.

⑫

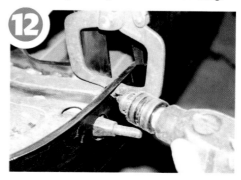

Once satisfied with rear panel's position in relation to boot floor and tailgate, Neil drilled 2mm holes by each pair of clamps. These holes will be used to hold on panel with self-tapping screws.

replacement tailgate and adjusted its alignment to match that of the original.

The tailgate's position is adjustable by adding or removing shims from between the gate and hinge. Adding a shim brings the tailgate up and out slightly, removing a shim takes it down and in. Why does one shim move the tailgate in two directions? I hear you ask. Because the tailgate slopes and the hinges are mounted at an angle.

The replacement tailgate will remain on the car until the rear panel and rear wings are installed and welded up, after which it will be removed again for overhaul.

Although we attached the rear panel firmly using self-tapping screws, we didn't weld it on at this stage. That will be done at the same time as the new rear wings are fitted — just in case any fine-tuning realignment is needed to make the rear panel line up with them and the tailgate.

In practice it usually does with little or no further repositioning, but it's frustrating and more than a little irritating when it won't and you've already welded the panel on!

Self-tappers have the advantage of allowing a panel's position to be changed slightly if you loosen them a little, but will hold it firmly if they're tightened.

After next issue's installment the project MGB's rear end should start to take on the appearance of a real car again. That's because we'll be fitting new rear wings, after preparation and localised repair work on the areas underneath them.

NEXT ISSUE
Fitting new rear wings

TAILGATE SWAP

Self-tappers hold panel firmly when tight, but you can vary the position if required by loosening them. This allows panel's position to be tweaked slightly if necessary when aligning the rear wings.

Time to change tailgates. As our car had some thick coats of paint which would affect alignment, the first job was to grind back to bare metal all round tailgate aperture. Don't forget your gloves.

Fitting a new tailgate rubber surround can be time-consuming if you're not used to it. The secret is to work round, pressing one side into channel, then levering other in with a screwdriver.

Replacement tailgate isn't perfect and will require lower edge attention, but it was temporarily aligned and fitted. This is easier with glass out, but don't remove it unless it needs replacing.

Tailgate is attached by four large cross-headed screws; two in each hinge. Fitting the gate is a two or preferably three-person job — you won't be able to support it and put screws in at same time.

How it looked first time. Top edge is too low — it should be flush with roof. It was also out at bottom. You can see how thick the various layers of paint on our car were, and how paint could affect fit.

No problem, you fit a shim (or two) between hinge and door frame. Make them from sheet steel if you can't get originals. Sometimes one hinge will need shimming but not other to achieve correct fit.

To achieve the final position (at least until rear wings are on) you have to latch the tailgate shut. This means fitting the lock ring. The threaded holes might need paint clearing out with a tap.

After fitting new tailgate we noticed that rear panel outer edges were slightly lower than they should have been. This was corrected by a couple of sharp hammer blows through a wooden block.

MGB GT

TIME REQUIRED **2 DAYS**

WORKSHOP RATING

Part fifteen: bodywork repairs are nearly finished. This time we replace the rear wing and outer wheelarch. Peter Simpson explains how.

The MGB HIVE

The project car featured on these pages belongs to and is being restored by the MGB Hive of Parsons Drove, Cambs.

The MG will be for sale when work is completed. If you are interested in buying the car, or just want to see how work is progressing, contact proprietor Nigel Petch (01945 700500). He says that readers are always welcome.

As well as being the region's leading supplier of MGB parts, the company undertakes servicing and repairs along with restoration work at their Fenland premises near Wisbech.

LAST issue, we left our 1971 MGB GT project car with the rear panel aligned and screwed in place. Final welding was being left until the rear wings were fitted. And that, along with installing the outer wheelarch section, is our mission this time.

First, a warning. From the picture sequence it might appear that our bodywork guru Neil Fincham put the rear wing on, jiggled it a bit and it fitted. In reality he made two attempts (the rear inner support and rear panel join needed adjustment after the first trial-fitting). But for those of us who don't spend our working lives sorting out MGBs, the wing will probably be on and off several times while adjustments are made to the supporting pieces behind.

When attempting to make the rear wing fit,

don't disturb the door or rear panel unless you're certain they are the cause of the panel's misalignment — which is unlikely if you've followed the procedures outlined in this series correctly. Once you move panels, it's easy to lose your reference points, making final alignment almost impossible. If you are sure the panels need moving, adjust one at a time, and mark your starting position so you can return the panel to it if necessary.

One problem emerged when we attempted to line up the wing. With everything else fitting perfectly, the front lower section was 8mm proud of the sill, of which it should effectively form a continuation. This is common with remanufactured MGB rear wings.

If the wing is only slightly proud, you can make it fit using a few careful hammer blows

and a block of wood to spread the load. This usually pulls the top in sufficiently, but leaves the curved bottom section still standing proud. If so, the panel is too big and the only solution is to unclip the bottom, and cut a strip out of the joining tab. Then reshape the tab to its original size from the panel base, leaving the curved section smaller.

Do this with the wing in place and the top joins tack-welded — it's easier to assess how much cutting and forming is required.

This time I haven't dealt with the preparation of surfaces to be joined (we've covered it already in this series). Basically make sure everything to be joined is straight, clean and clear of all rust, paint and grease.

You must also protect the welded joints, otherwise moisture will get in, causing rapid

REPLACING REAR WING/WHEELARCH

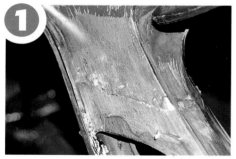

1 First we removed remaining bits of wing, starting at the top. This joint is leaded on chrome-bumper MGBs like ours, and had to be melted with blowtorch. Removing lead is easy, putting it back isn't.

2 I once mentioned that Heritage MGB rear wings were being supplied without the C-post section. Apparently this was a faulty batch and they are supplied complete, so Neil removed the old C-post.

3 After drilling through spot welds attaching inner edge, Neil used his custom-built wide-reach hacksaw to chop through top joint. As bottom edge was already disconnected, panel could be twisted off.

7 If you're not an originality fetishist, you can make life a lot easier by modifying the new wing slightly, for example, by snipping out this small corner section that should sit underneath the door pillar.

8 It's also a lot easier to fit the wing if you cut most of this tuck-under section away from top of rear pillar. The joint is leaded (on chrome bumper models) or covered by a badge (rubber bumper).

9 Trial fitting the new wing. Door has to be on and positioned correctly (see May 1995), to use it as a reference point. Align the door and wing swage lines, and strive for even panel gaps of about 5mm.

Neil Fincham from the MGB Hive contemplates the project GT's rear wing, wondering how long it's going to take to fit this one.

...orrosion. I paint the seams with weld-through primer, although many people use seam-sealer mastic over the joint. This stops water getting in, rather than preventing damage once it's there. Perhaps the best idea is to use both?

Protect inside the panels too — remember that factory primer is meant only to keep the panels rust-free during storage. The MGB Hive paint them with Hammerite.

We're almost at the end of the body metalwork restoration. Next issue we'll fit the front wings and do some tidying up. Then

TOOLS REQUIRED

● Drill, drill bits and metal scriber
● Welder (preferably MIG) and four sets of welding clamps
● Hacksaw, tin snips, panel hammer and wooden block

we'll be following the mechanical overhaul for a few months, while Neil catches up with repairs on the other side of the bodyshell.

4 ...emoving paint from gutter allowed Neil to find ...d drill spot welds. He also cut top of wing (under ...aded join) here. Channel was twisted away, but ...ilgate support strut was deliberately left in place.

5 Neil drilled out the holes in rear inner wing/support frame so the new panel could be plug-welded from underneath. Don't worry about sticking to original weld positions, these varied during production.

6 On chrome bumper cars, join between rear wing and rear panel was leaded. To make joining easier you can twist rear panel edge flush then set it back using a joddler so the rear wing's edge sits on top.

10 ...his is how cut-out piece fits into door pillar — if ...ou leave panel as supplied it must slip up and ...etween inner wing and window pillar. This method ...easier and window surround will hide the join.

11 With front, top and back aligned correctly, bottom edge was 6-7mm proud of sill — a common problem with MGB rear wings. You might make it fit like this, but we had to modify the joining tab.

12 At the back Neil bent tab flat. When satisfied with wing's position, he drilled two holes through join and inserted screws. Rear panel, if you remember last time, was screwed in place only at this stage. ▶

NEXT ISSUE
FITTING FRONT WING

REPLACING REAR WING/WHEELARCH

13 Wing was tack-welded alongside clamps and to where it meets inner sill. Wing needs attaching semi-permanently before next stage, but tack-welding is used in case position needs changing.

14 Outer section of inner wheelarch slips straight up under wing and is attached to prepared inner arch and outer wing lip. Protect inside first — the MGB Hive use Hammerite for all internal work.

15 Clamp inner wheelarch to wing, using squares of metal to prevent clamps damaging wing. Drill holes 4in apart round wing lip so you can plug-weld through. Make extra closing panel for sill end

16 Neil used wet paper towels to cool area and prevent wing distorting. Start in centre, then do one side at a time. Repeat on join to inner wheelarch, then seam-weld. Yes, Neil should wear overalls.

17 Time to fix the wing. Start with easy bit, the top seam which will be under window surround. Drill holes an inch apart and plug-weld. Welds will need grinding afterwards so screen rubber can fit on.

18 C-post section is attached similarly, except here the wing is not drilled, only backing. Then move inside car and weld through to inner arch, tack-welding first, then seam-welding. Access is tight

19 At rear, arch is joined to boot floor extension piece we fitted in August. There's not much room but it's easier if you start at outer (wing) side and work inwards forming another continuous seam.

20 Weld back panel to wing after trimming flange to size. Fixing panel left a small gap at top, which was filled with a sliver of metal welded in. Don't forget the join lower down, where bumper sits.

21 Neil welded wing rear edge to the inner by plug-welding through holes we saw drilled in step five. He ended up with a gap at top of channel section, which he filled with two fillets of metal welded in

22 There will also be a hole in window aperture bottom corner that requires localised repair. Here you have to form a repair section from two pieces. Shape inner piece like this and weld it to outer and inner wing.

23 Then, using piece you've fitted as template, cut a widened C-shaped piece to form outer closing section. Cut-and-let-in techniques are easy with practice, but expect to waste some metal at first.

24 Door pillar bottom edge, which was removed with old wing, needs remaking. Start with front edge, then cut an appropriately-shaped strip to close panel. Weld it, then dress with grinder to finish.

MGB GT

Part sixteen: to conclude the bodywork restoration of our MGB GT project car, Peter Simpson covers fitting new front wings.

DOESN'T time fly when you're having fun. It's taken us over a year to cover the body restoration of our MGB GT project car, and this time we complete the last lap — fitting a front wing.

These wings bolt on, which makes fitting much easier. You can also carry out fine adjustments to a bolt-on panel's position if you slacken the bolts slightly, move the panel and then retighten. With welded panels, once you've started welding you're committed to that precise position.

Although fitting MGB front wings is quite easy compared with some body work, it's well worth taking time and trouble over it so you get the fit exactly right, as any inconsistencies (particularly in the wing/bonnet gap) will be very visible.

You have a choice of Heritage wings made on the original MG tooling and costing around £170, or reproduction wings which are about £65 cheaper.

Both are made from the same gauge metal but, as you would expect, the reproduction panels do usually require more fettling, and therefore probably take an extra one or two hours to fit. However there's no reason why they can't be made to look just as good as original equipment (OE) wings, provided you take the necessary time and trouble.

Like most reputable restorers, the MGB Hive normally use genuine panels (when they're available) on all in-house work and on customer's cars unless the car owner specifically requests reproduction parts.

However, even genuine wings frequently require some fettling to make them fit properly. You may have to attach and remove

them several times to make the necessary adjustments.

If, like us, you're fitting original wings, bear in mind that these now come coated with cathodic primer. This shouldn't be removed (except locally where necessary to correct faults) as the primer is an important part of the panel's corrosion protection. The only preparation necessary is light roughening of the surface to provide a key.

Whatever type of wing you use though, the underside will need protecting. Even cathodic primer won't provide long-term protection on its own. The MGB Hive use Hammerite, but there are other products on the market, which provide lasting protection.

As you can see, our genuine wing went on with relatively little difficulty. However, you might come across other problems. Things to

watch out for are a wing that's too high at the back (you can sometimes cure this by taking a strip of metal out of the bottom edge and reshaping), uneven back edge (cure by trimming or shaping as long as there's enough metal to do this) and minor dents and knocks caused during transit. You may also come across unevenness in the mating surfaces, which stops the panel sitting properly.

MGB Hive bodywork specialist Neil Fincham trial-fits the new front wing for the first time.

FITTING NEW FRONT WINGS

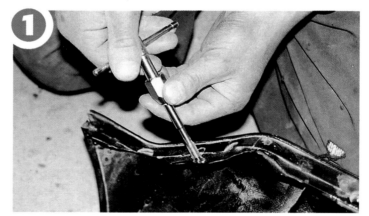

1

Neil had to clear paint from two threaded holes in back of wing. Use appropriate-sized tap if you have one, if not hacksaw a cross in an appropriate size bolt thread and use that as a tap.

The MGB HIVE

The project car featured on these pages belongs to and is being restored by the **MGB Hive** of Parsons Drove, Cambs.

The MG will be for sale when work is completed. If you are interested in buying the car, or just want to see how work is progressing, contact MGB Hive proprietor **Nigel Petch (01945 700500)**. He says that *Practical Classics* readers are always welcome.

As well as being the region's leading supplier of MGB parts, the company undertakes servicing and repairs along with restoration work at their Fenland premises near Wisbech.

5

Fixing kit comes with three different types of washer. Circular ones go along the top, but the back two bolts have rectangular washers. Don't forget the small spring washers between bolt head and washer.

obvious faults on delivery and again before dispatch (I know the MGB Hive do this because Neil is sometimes called away from work on our car to check panels). However, in some instances you can't tell if something will fit unless it's bolted on to a car.

The wings are attached by a line of bolts along the top edge — the ones you can see when the bonnet is opened. There are also two bolts attaching the wing's trailing edge to the door post. These can be reached from underneath the dashboard. Two further bolts attach the front end and are accessed from behind the radiator grille.

Finally, there are three bolts along the bottom edge, attaching the wing's bottom to the sill structure.

There is also a sealing strip which goes along the rear edge between the wing and windscreen support panel. This has to be replaced along with the wing and, as you can see from the picture sequence, the easiest way of doing it is to attach the strip to the wing first. Then its shape is finally moulded by the windscreen support, which is much more sturdy.

TOOLS REQUIRED

- Drill, drill bits and metal scriber
- ½in AF spanner
- Welding clamps
- Small hammer and block of wood
- Body tools for panel reshaping

USEFUL BACK ISSUES

- Our MGB GT restoration started in the September 1994 issue when we introduced the car and advised on buying one.
- October 1994: stripdown starts and front wings are removed.
- November 1994: further stripping, including glass and fuel tank.
- December 1994: sill, floorpan and cross-member removal.
- January 1995: front chassis leg and under-floor rear spring mount repairs.
- February 1995: repairs to outer edge of front bulkhead.
- March 1995: fitting new inner sill, castle section, crossmember and floorpan.
- April 1995: scuttle and windscreen support panel repairs.
- Spring 1995: inner wing, lower windscreen support sections and bulkhead closing panel.
- May 1995: fitting new centre and outer sills.
- June 1995: fitting a new oil cooler panel.
- July 1995: spring hanger repairs.
- August 1995: chassis leg repairs and boot floor removal.
- September 1995: false boot floor and rear panel fitting.
- October 1995: fitting rear wings.

Copies of these magazines are available from our Back Issues department, details on page 27.

Most faults like this can be cured easily. ⌐ome cannot. If, for example, the panel is too ⌐ort at the top, the top curve is too shallow ⌐ the headlamp aperture is the wrong shape ⌐heck it against the bezel), rectification will ⌐e difficult if not impossible.

In these circumstances return the panel to ⌐e suppliers and ask them to send one that ⌐ts. Reputable suppliers check panels for

⌐t this sealing strip around closing panel before ⌐e wing's first trial fitting. That's important ⌐ecause the rubber contacts the wing and will ⌐erefore push it out slightly, affecting its fit.

First trial fitting. Clamp the front edge and secure at bulkhead end of wing with two bolts. Align this edge with the bonnet. Aim for an even gap from front to rear. Compare width with opposite wing.

If, like us, you've replaced the inner wing top section, you may well find that the bolt holes don't line up exactly. Don't be too concerned, it's easy enough to enlarge the holes slightly with a drill.

Then with all the bolts so far fitted, gripping the wing (but not so tight it can't be moved) check alignment. As well as checking for even panel gaps, make sure the wing/door swage line is even.

⌐ird type of washer with rounded ends are used ⌐ere, to secure the bolts which go through the ⌐ulkhead into the wing. Access is from underneath ⌐e dashboard. Yes, being a contortionist helps!

NEXT ISSUE
ENGINE REMOVAL

FITTING NEW FRONT WINGS

8 You would also normally attach the wing's bottom rear edge using three bolts at this stage. Unfortunately, we couldn't, because the lower edge was standing 4-5mm proud of the sill.

9 That was the only visible fault though, so off came the wing for rectification. The cause turned out to be a little excess metal at the top, but its effect was magnified at the bottom edge.

10 Then Neil trial-fitted the wing again. Ours was fine this time, but many will need further tweaking, which involves another removal and refit. Then remove wing and seam-seal all the joints.

11 First part of the final fitting. Note the sealing strip stuck along the wing's edge to make a watertight joint with the windscreen support panel. Have all fixings ready to hand — that wing is heavy!

12 This is how you reach those awkward rear mounting screws — it's a bit easier with the glovebox inner lining out. Offside is slightly more awkward as wiper motor has to come out.

13 It's easiest to fit all the top edge bolts loosely and then tighten them down a little at a time in sequence, starting from windscreen end. Check and adjust panel's fit as you go if necessary.

14 The two front-end bolts fit into these captive nuts. As you can see, this part of the wing rarely lines up on its own, hence the use of grips during the initial fitting-up to pull it into position.

15 Neil uses the front wishbone as a fulcrum point to fine-tune the rear wing/door panel gap. It looks crude but it's very effective. Aim for an even gap. Check door opens without fouling the wing edge.

16 This is how you get wing-to-body sealing strip to sit properly — the wood's there to stop the hammer blows from marking the strip. Don't hit it hard — a couple of light taps should be enough.

17 And here it is sitting properly. As you can see, the strip is supposed to extend slightly (2-3mm) forward of the windscreen support panel. This is to allow for slight contraction during service.

18 At bottom rear edge of wing, three bolts go into captive nuts in sill structure behind. Many owners don't know this as captive nuts often rot out, and the wing lower edge may have been welded on.

19 Finished at last! It's well worth taking plenty of time and trouble getting the panel gaps right when bolting on front wings. How well they fit has a big influence on how good whole car looks.

MGB GT

WORKSHOP RATING

TIME REQUIRED 3-5 hours

C C C C

Part seventeen: with all the body panels sorted out, Peter Simpson gets on with the mechanical overhaul. He starts by removing the engine.

John Lakey, the MGB Hive's chief mechanic, manoeuvres our MGB's engine out and away.

ARE YOU wary of removing an engine? Well don't be; the job is a lot easier than some people imagine.

It's not usually that time-consuming either. Our MGB's engine was out and ready to be worked on within four hours, and I can't see it taking a novice much longer. Refitting can be a different matter though, as we'll see in a few issues time.

Don't worry about not having an engine crane — it's more cost-effective for most enthusiasts to hire one as and when required. A typical hire charge is around £25 for a

weekend — most hire shops do special weekend deals — and with decent cranes costing at least £200, buying isn't justified for occasional use.

LIFTING TACKLE

THE hire shop will require proof of identity and your address, plus a deposit to cover loss or damage during the hire. If you're at all unsure how the thing operates, do ask before leaving the shop.

As you've probably spotted already, John Lakey of the MGB Hive used a stout rope to lift the engine. Surely he should have used a chain? Not necessarily, good examples of either will do.

A hired engine crane will usually come complete with lifting tackle. If it does, use it — the hirer will have made sure it's up to the job. Otherwise I'd use a good quality car tow rope (not the 99p type you buy from car boot sales) as anything that's up to taking the rolling weight of a complete car being pulled uphill should be able to tackle an engine, especially when each length is, in effect, bearing 25 per cent of the total weight.

Alternatively, yachting and boat chandlers supply good-quality rope. For safety's sake go for at least three-ton breaking strain. Inspect the rope thoroughly (especially if it's

been used before), and reject one with any damage, cuts, split strands or even excessive oil contamination.

The MGB Hive's method of attachment might raise one or two eyebrows, but it's commonly used throughout the motor trade and is no more risky than the factory method of lifting BMC B-series engines (by an eye bolted to each of two studs screwed into the cylinder head). At the back it's a lot more secure, as there's no way the rope can come out of that channel between the back plate and engine block.

SPREAD THE LOAD

AT THE front, John looped the rope around the back of the water pump body (tuck it behind the alternator lug to keep it back), taking care not to foul the water pipes. This is less satisfactory but most of the weight is at the back, and at least the front load is spread around three bolts and a mounting stud. A further advantage of attaching the lifting gear further down like this is that the engine cannot swing when it's moved on the crane.

Avoid looping a rope around any tight corners where there's a chance of anything cutting or fraying it when it takes the strain. Use a thick cloth or similar where it's in contact with anything at all sharp. The ends must be tied firmly together too, and looped so that if one or two lengths do break, the engine will remain suspended from the others. Former Boy Scouts will know that a reef knot is suitable (left over right and right over left).

Ensure you're not in any danger should the engine fall. This is particularly important in the early stages when you can easily put your hands or fingers somewhere that's trappable while freeing the engine from its mounts. Use a lever or large screwdriver if a mounting rubber or similar needs shifting, keeping your hands well out of the way. A falling engine could easily take your hand off — you have been warned!

Lifting the engine out is really a two person job, one to operate the crane, the other to manoeuvre the engine free while directing the crane operator.

You'll notice that the engine — still covered in dust from the body repairs — was stripped of most ancillaries before being removed from the car. That's not essential, it will come out with the carburettors, alternator and distributor still attached. But it's best to do it this way if the engine is to be worked on. They'll have to come off eventually anyway, and doing it now reduces the weight being lifted. You can also exert more leverage on stiff nuts and bolts while the engine is fixed in place.

The procedure shown here is for chrome-bumpered MGBs. On all but the very first rubber-bumpered models the radiator is mounted further forward and doesn't have to come out during engine removal.

The engine mounts are also different and attach to the engine's front plate rather than the block itself. The best way of disconnecting these is to remove the two nuts securing the mounts to the plate. Do not remove the

TOOLS REQUIRED

- Engine crane (1½ tons minimum), stout rope
- ⁷⁄₁₆, ½ and ⁹⁄₁₆ AF spanners (two of each)
- Crosshead and flathead screwdrivers
- An assistant
- Large lever to separate engine and gearbox
- Trolley jack

bolts though, until the engine's weight is on the crane. Then the engine can be pulled forward and out.

The work shown here was done by two people. Apprentice mechanic Michael Banstead did the initial stripping-out, and chief mechanic John Lakey appeared for the safety-critical lift, with Michael watching (and learning).

Michael started by jacking up the front end and placing a pair of axle stands under the crossmember. This was to give him room to get underneath and tackle the bottom bellhousing and starter motor bolts. Just before lifting the trolley jack was used again, to raise the gearbox into the transmission tunnel.

You can also remove the engine with the gearbox attached, but in view of the increased weight and bulk, separating the two components is probably the best bet for most owners.

Next time, we'll be starting the engine overhaul. Obviously that will be useful not only to MGB owners, but to anyone with a BMC B-series powered car.

USEFUL BACK ISSUES

Copies of these magazines are available from our Back Issues department, details on page 3.

ENGINE OUT

1 Work on one side of the car at a time. Michael started by disconnecting the carburettor fuel feeds. Plug pipes or drain tank first. Our tank had previously been removed and the coolant drained.

2 Next remove the carburettor/inlet manifold spacing blocks by levering away like this. Then remove the heat shield. The spacing blocks can perish and split — order new ones if necessary.

3 Inlet and exhaust manifolds are separate on BMC B-series engines, but share mounting bolts. They're ½in AF and sometimes tight. Exhaust pipe had been removed to facilitate body repairs.

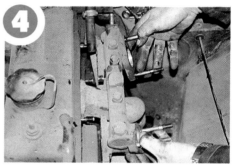

4 After disconnecting the brake servo vacuum feed pipe (at top of picture, between manifold and head) Michael pulled the inlet manifold off its studs and out, followed by the exhaust manifold.

5 Now you can tackle the nearside engine mount. First undo two top nuts (½in AF) and lift covering plate off. This is often missing. Rubber-bumpered MGB mountings are different — see the text.

6 Then undo the four lower nuts (½in AF), but leave the bolts in place at this stage. This is perfectly safe as the engine's weight bearing down on the mount will ensure that it cannot move.

7 Next tackle accessible nearside bellhousing bolts (½in AF). Top two bolts go into block from other side and usually have to be attacked with a spanner rather than socket due to restricted clearance.

8 Moving across to the offside, first thing to take off is the HT lead assembly; ours went straight in the scrap bin. Use new parts on reassembly unless the old cap and leads really are perfect.

NEXT ISSUE
ENGINE STRIPDOWN

ENGINE OUT

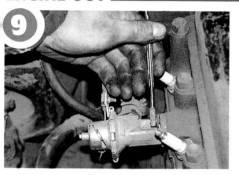

9 MGB heater control valve is delicate, so take care when pulling hose off from behind. Then unbolt from block (two ⁷⁄₁₆in AF bolts). Inspect internals and use a new one on reassembly if it's corroded.

10 Oil cooler pipes are disconnected from block and filter housing next (⁵⁄₈in AF). Seal pipe ends to prevent oil spillage. Re-using old pipes and cooler is false economy after extensive engine work.

11 To provide room to swing engine forward, radiator and support panel must come out. Disconnect top and bottom hoses (prepare for coolant spillage) then undo ½in AF bolts each side to release panel.

12 To disconnect temperature gauge undo locking nut and withdraw element like this. Go easy as capillary tube from the sensor snaps easily, especially when being disturbed for first time in years.

13 Alternator mounting is the universal three bolt set-up. Slacken all three slightly first, then move alternator towards engine to release fan belt, remove nuts and bolts and take alternator off.

14 Starter motor can come out now. First disconnect power feed cable. Motor is held on by two ⁵⁄₁₆in AF bolts. One can be reached easily enough from on top, but you have to get under car for other.

15 Go underneath and tackle other starter motor bolt. For safety you should also undo the four bell-housing bolts underneath, while engine and box are held together. You'll need two ½in AF spanners.

16 Now the only fixed mounts holding engine in are remaining bellhousing bolts. One offside bolt, shown here, is too long to come out completely with the engine in: knock it clear of engine using a drift.

17 As explained in text, the **MGB Hive** prefer to use a strong rope when lifting elderly engines. Get crane head close to rocker cover, then attach rope through cast hole on back of block like this.

18 At front, thread rope around under water pump housing exactly as shown here. Get rope back against block, and ensure it won't damage delicate water pipe on right when strain is taken up.

19 Now, after tying rope ends firmly together, lift crane jib slightly to take strain. Check all ropes are okay and lift further. Once free to move forward, lever engine and gearbox apart like this.

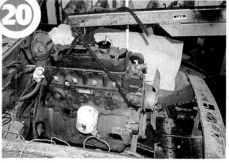

20 Once free of the gearbox, engine should lift out without difficulty unless you've forgotten something. Keep an eye on ropes at all times, keep clear and raise engine no higher than necessary.

MGB GT

WORKSHOP RATING

TIME REQUIRED
5-6 hours

C C C C C

Part eighteen: Peter Simpson starts stripping — but don't look away, he's just working on an MGB engine.

OVER the next three or four issues, we'll be stripping, overhauling and rebuilding an MGB engine. I'd better come clean and admit the engine we're working on isn't the one from our car. As the more sharp-eyed MGB experts will have spotted already, it's from a rubber-bumpered MGB — the engine mountings are different.

The reason we've changed units is simple — ours was too good. The car was bought as an MoT test failure, and its engine turned out to be almost perfect. While this was undoubtedly good news for the MGB Hive, an engine with virtually nothing wrong with it wasn't a lot of use to us. So we decided to demonstrate stripdown and rebuilding techniques on another engine from the MGB Hive's stockpile. This unit's exact history isn't known, but it was thought to have bottom-end problems.

When an engine requires overhauling, you've several options. One is to simply buy a service exchange unit and fit that. Because you get a complete lump in one this is certainly the simplest method, but the labour has to be paid for somewhere, so unless your engine needs a lot of work, a full recon engine is unlikely to be the cheapest option. It will, however, come with a worthwhile guarantee, assuming that it's from a reputable supplier.

Short engines are also available from most engine suppliers, and are worth considering if you don't object to some dismantling work. Basically, a short engine is complete from the top of the cylinder block down (block,

Norman, the MGB Hive's resident engine man, hard at work.

crankshaft, pistons and bearings, plus the camshaft assembly on an overhead valve unit like the MGB) although many exclude the oil sump. Some also come without an oil pump — exact specifications vary according to supplier, and are worth checking.

The major component not included — the head — is the bit that's easiest to overhaul yourself anyway. Again, a short engine will come with a guarantee, though naturally it

ENGINE STRIPDOWN

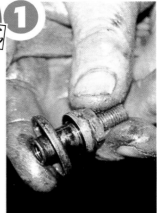

1 First job is to take the rocker cover off using a ½in AF spanner. Nuts attach directly to the outer two rocker shaft studs. Two different lengths of stud are used — the longer two at either end.

5 If head isn't yet free, it's likely that one or more stud is rusted in. Tapping on top of a suspected stud often helps free it, but you must use a soft-headed hammer to avoid damaging threads.

9 After removing head studs using a stud remover or the two-nut technique (see text), invert the block and undo bolts securing front plate and timing cover. Remove cover, but not front plate.

TOOLS REQUIRED

- ⁷⁄₁₆in and ½in AF spanners/sockets
- 33mm socket and extension bar
- Copper-faced hammer (Thor or similar)
- Cold chisel at least 1in wide
- Two long, good quality screwdrivers, ½in blade minimum

won't cover defects caused by your duff assembly work.

The third option is to dismantle it yourse send the wearing parts away for inspection and possibly machining, and then

...xt slacken the head nuts — in order given in ...rkshop manual. Release outer two rocker-only ...s, so the valve springs' pressure against the ...ck helps break the head gasket seal.

Pushing a screwdriver between block and head to free the head isn't recommended (you risk damaging the mating surfaces) but you can lever between these two casting lugs like this.

Next job was to undo the remaining two rocker stud nuts and lift the gear off complete. There should be a shim under each rocker pedestal, but many engines have lost theirs over the years.

...e's another place you can attack a stubborn ...d, but again you must use a soft-headed ...mmer to avoid damaging the head casting. The ...ter pump has to come off first to give access.

With the head off you can inspect the bores. Look for a wear ridge around the top of the upper piston ring's travel. If you can feel any wear, a rebore's needed. If in doubt, have it bored.

Now for some simple spanner work removing the engine side covers. The front one, shown here, incorporates the wire-mesh crankcase breather filter mesh. Replace this as a matter of course.

...n oil thrower disc until its cutout aligns with ...crankshaft's woodruff key, and lift off. Then ...do the 18 sump securing bolts — all ⁷⁄₁₆in AF. ...e care not to lose the washers underneath.

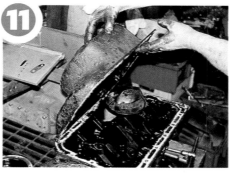

Sump pan might be a little tight, especially if anyone's been using instant gasket to stop leaks. Once the sump was off it became quite obvious what had happened inside this engine!

Badly mishapen oil pump pick-up strainer was the clue. It must have become blocked and then, when it couldn't suck oil, tried to suck the gauze inside out. Result: no oil getting through.

...ssemble. This is usually the cheapest ...proach as you'll be doing all the time-...suming work yourself rather than paying ...neone else. The big drawback is that ...y'll effectively be little or no guarantee — ...onditioners will be liable only if you can ...ieve the almost impossible and prove a ...ect is down to their poor workmanship. ...ometimes though, if an engine requires a ...of work, the DIY route won't save you ...ch money. You'll probably have some idea ...what a unit's like inside from how it runs, ...of course you won't know for certain until ...1've partially stripped it. All the same, this ...he approach adopted by most competent

DIY repairers and it's therefore the method of working we'll be following here.

Start by thoroughly degreasing the outside. This makes dismantling easier and a lot more pleasant. And don't forget to drain the oil sump. Even after you've done this there will be some fluids left inside the engine, so be prepared for a cascade whenever the engine is turned over.

As the engine comes apart, you'll be making decisions about what can and cannot be reused. Some parts which should be replaced as a matter of course are identified in the picture captions. Additionally, we recommend changing the rocker shaft,

The MGB HIVE

THE project car featured on these pages belongs to and is being restored by the MGB Hive of Parsons Drove, Cambs. The MG will be for sale when work is completed.

If you are interested in buying the car, or just want to see how work is progressing, contact MGB Hive proprietor Nigel Petch (01945 700500). He says that *Practical Classics* readers are always welcome to the workshop.

As well as being the region's leading supplier of MGB parts, the company undertakes servicing and repairs along with restoration work at their Fenland premises near Wisbech.

NEXT ISSUE STRIPPING & ASSESSING THE ENGINE

ENGINE STRIPDOWN

bushes and nuts, plus of course all gaskets. I'd also strongly advise having the engine rebored unless you're absolutely certain bore wear is within limits — bear in mind the amount of dismantling required to reach them.

Like most reputable rebuilders, the MGB Hive based in Cambridgeshire always replace all cam followers (and fit a new or reprofiled cam) during rebuilds. They also check that the pushrods are straight by rolling them along a flat surface. Keep those pushrods in the correct order as well.

It's also important to retain the rocker shaft position locking tab. This tab prevents the shaft from turning in service, which would upset its oil feed. It is underneath one of the rocker nuts and is easily lost.

In caption nine I mention the two nut technique for removing studs. This works thus: put two nuts onto the threaded part of the stud being removed, tight up against each other. Then try to turn the lower one. This usually draws the stud out. If it doesn't work try again with the nuts tighter together.

We're covering the dismantling in two parts. This month we're looking at the work up to and including timing gear removal — most of which is relevant whether you're fitting a short engine or doing the whole job yourself. Next time, we'll finish dismantling and look at how to decide what does, and what doesn't need work.

USEFUL BACK ISSUES

Copies of these magazines are available from our Back Issues department, details on page 3.

Oil pump is held on by three ½in **AF** bolts. Remove them, lift the pump body off and then remove the studs. Failed oil pump can cause immense damage so it's best to fit a new one.

To undo the camshaft sprocket nut, lock engine using brass drift in crank gear as shown. Then tackle the nut with 33mm socket and long extension bar — this nut is usually very tight.

Removing the timing chain. Lever the crankshaft pulley forward until it touches the woodruff key, using a couple of strong screwdrivers. You don't actually need to remove the woodruff key.

Undo the three ⅞in **AF** camshaft retaining plate bolts. Again, there are sprung locking washers behind the bolt heads — retain them all for reuse on reassembly. Leave camshaft in place for now.

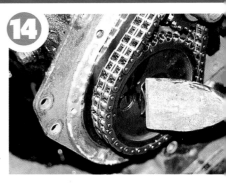

Returning now to the timing gear, first flatten camshaft sprocket locking tab using a large flat chisel. Locking tabs should be used once only as bending and straightening weakens them.

Undo two ⅞in bolts to release the timing chain tensioner assembly. Replace everything except the bolts. If your tensioner bolts have spring washers replace them with shakeproof ones.

You can then use the same technique to lever the cam sprocket off. There will be enough sideway movement in the chain for the sprocket to come off. New timing chains are only about £6.

Camshaft retaining bolts are also the final fixing for the engine front plate, which can now be carefully tapped off. Avoid levering it off. We'll finish dismantling the engine next time...

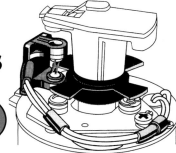

MGB GT

WORKSHOP RATING

TIME REQUIRED
3-5 hours

C C C C C

Part nineteen: Peter Simpson concludes the engine stripdown and assesses for wear.

LAST TIME, we left our MGB engine minus head, sump and most ancillaries, but with the camshaft, pistons and crank still firmly attached to the block. In other words we left it as a 'short' unit. Now we're concluding the stripdown and assessment for wear.

Even though the components will have to be refurbished by professionals, it's important to get an idea of what's going to want doing so that you can decide whether to go ahead or bolt it all back together and buy a service-exchange unit. If it needs a lot of work, and you're not bothered about having a different engine this might well be more cost-effective — but do check specifications, because how much of a reconditioned engine has actually been reconditioned can vary enormously.

Many reuse, repair or replace decisions are commonsense. But imagine for one moment just how annoyed you'd feel if forced to do the whole job again in six-months time simply because something you decided was just about reusable turned out not to be. If in doubt, always replace.

DISMANTLING

THE picture-sequence covers the main stages of stripping the short block, but there are just a few additional points to note. First, on all GB prefix and later engines (check the engine number plate) the distributor drive can be removed (pictures 2-4) only when the engine is set to 90 degrees before or after top-dead-centre (TDC). This is dead-easy to find — it's

when all four pistons are the same height in their bores.

As you can see Norman used his trusty Thor copper-headed mallet several times. Th is designed for shifting hard-to-move compo-

ENGINE STRIPDOWN

1 Starting where we left off last time, with the engine front plate about to succumb to a couple of carefully-placed mallet blows. Make sure everything is completely undone first!

2 Take out the distributor driveshaft which meshes with the cam at this stage. To do this first set the engine to **90 degrees** fore or aft of top-dead-centre (TDC). Then undo the countersunk screw.

3 Then you can slide the distributor drive retaining ring assembly out. It's a tight fit in the block and may be slightly stiff. Try twisting it slightly which may help to free it, while exerting a constant pul

4 Here's a sneaky way of extracting the driveshaft. Screw one of the oil pump or tappet cover studs, removed last time, into the thread on the end of the shaft and pull. Shaft will turn as it comes out.

5 Time to start extracting pistons! With a 33mm (1¼in AF) socket turn the camshaft until pistons to be tackled first are at the bottom of their bores, so the big-end bolts can be reached easily.

6 Next undo the locking nuts using a ½in AF socket. Contrary to popular belief these locking nuts can be reused on reassembly provided, of course, that they are completely undamaged.

TOOLS REQUIRED

- **Copper-headed mallet and Brass drift**
- **Flathead screwdriver, 7⁄16in, ½in, 9⁄16in and 1¼in AF (33mm) ring spanners or sockets**
- **Plenty of hand-cleaner**

The MGB HIVE

THE project car featured on these pages belongs to and is being restored by the MGB Hive of Parsons Drove, Cambs. The MG will be for sale when work is completed.

If you are interested in buying the car, or just want to see how work is progressing, contact MGB Hive proprietor Nigel Petch (01945 700500). He says that *Practical Classics* readers are always welcome to the workshop.

As well as being the region's leading supplier of MGB parts, the company undertakes servicing and repairs along with restoration work at their Fenland premises near Wisbech.

drift to shift reluctant components — the chances of causing permanent damage are just too great. This is particularly important once you've started removing the piston/conrod assemblies revealing the polished crankshaft journals.

Although the crank itself is a hefty, solid lump of metal, the journals are machined to fine tolerances, and an inadvertent knock from even a copper hammer can mark the surface. You'll then have to grind a crank which might have been perfectly okay before you started! And a nick from a cold chisel may well be enough to write a crank off completely — especially one that's already been ground undersize.

Go easy on the conrod ends too. In particular, avoid hitting the mating surface between rod and cap as it's finely machined and if damaged the rod and cap will probably need replacing.

The other part of dismantling which demands special care is extracting the

camshaft. Here the danger is that the sharp edges of the cam lobes will mark the relatively soft camshaft bearings if allowed to pull across them. These bearings don't normally need replacing unless they've been damaged by careless dismantling, but if they do need doing it's quite a major job and one which has to be done by a machine shop with reaming and line-boring facilities.

You can avoid any chance of this happening by leaving camshaft removal until last, and drawing the front of the cam out with one hand while supporting the back with your other, twisting the camshaft slowly as you withdraw it.

◄ents without damaging them, but even so it ◄eeds to be used thoughtfully. Just a little too ◄uch force in the wrong place can cause ◄amage. And don't, whatever you do, use a ◄lid hammer or anything harder than a brass

7 ◄ow, using a soft brass drift or similar, gently ◄nock the bolt heads back. With luck, the ◄onrod and piston will move back up the bore ◄ightly at the same time as a result of this.

8 You can then lift the bearing cap off, along with the bearing inside thus exposing the first crankshaft journal. Be extra careful from now on not to inadvertently damage the crankshaft.

9 The time when you're most likely to inadvertently 'nick' the crank is now, when pushing the piston/conrod assembly up and out from underneath. It shouldn't need all that much force...

10 ◄ith all four piston assemblies out (don't forget ◄o twist crank half a turn after the first two) undo ◄ain bearing cap nuts using a 9⁄16in AF socket. Air ◄ower isn't essential, it's just quicker.

11 Caps are often very tight (especially the end ones) but again there's a crafty way of freeing it — pop one of the securing bolts into the vacant threaded centre hole and tap it sideways like this.

12 Front cap also has a handy lip on its bottom edge which can be used to tap it free — but only in conjunction with a brass drift as shown here. Don't hit it with any kind of hammer directly.

ASSESSING WEAR

HAVING come this far, it's a false economy to put back anything that isn't in perfect condition. Personally I'd almost always have the crank reground, and it will probably have to be done if the copper backing is showing through anywhere on any of the bearing surfaces. If the copper isn't showing through you might get away with just popping a new set of bearings in, but have the crank checked. The cost of a regrind (typically £40-£50) is a small price to pay for the peace of mind of a crank that's good as new.

On the camshaft it's the lobes which wear. Check the profile of the lobe: if the curvature is flattened, the lobe is worn. Exchange cams for MGBs aren't that expensive (about £35 for standard item) but bear in mind that if you replace the cam you'll have to fit new followers too. Be careful here because two different types of follower and pushrod were used on MGBs — I'll explain the differences when we start putting the thing back together.

Some components should be changed irrespective of condition. As well as crank bearings (including thrust washers), gaskets, oil seals etc, you should always replace pistons and rings, along with the timing chain and tensioner. I almost always pop a new oil pump in too, though not all professional reconditioners consider it necessary. We looked briefly at assessing bore wear last time, but basically your guide should be the wear ridge at the top of the top piston ring's travel (ie the join between the piece of bore which a ring contacts and the piece which it doesn't). If you can feel little or no ridge with your finger, the bore may well be okay (though again only a professional with proper measuring gear will be able to tell for sure), if not, a rebore is required.

IT'S A GRIND...

MGB CRANKSHAFT journals can be ground to 0.010in, 0.020in, 0.030in or 0.040in undersize, and 0.020in, 0.030in, 0.040in and 0.060in oversize pistons are available. This doesn't necessarily mean that, say, a 0.020in undersize crank has another two lives left. A badly scored or worn crank may well need 0.030in or even 0.040in taking out to make it round again. Similarly, a worn 0.030in bore may have to be taken to 0.060in to eliminate all wear.

Most people assume that an engine with oversize bores, bearings or pistons must have been overhauled at least once before. In most cases it will have, but it isn't 100 per cent certain. It wasn't unknown for manufacturers to machine slightly defective components oversize or undersize and then use them on new engines. Additionally, engine defects during warranty were usually rectified by fitting a factory reconditioned unit which might well include undersize or oversize components.

By next time, all the components which need refurbishing will have come back from the machine shop, and we'll be ready to start the big build-up.

ENGINE STRIPDOWN

The moment of truth — lifting the crankshaft out from the block. Prepare for a surprise if you've never done this before — crankshafts are a lot heavier than most people expect!

Finally, extract the camshaft — carefully twisting as you go. Support the back as it comes out so that the camshaft lobes don't contact the soft camshaft bearing surfaces in the block.

Checking camshafts for wear. The lobe on the right is good, the one on the left (notice how much flatter the curve on top is) is worn and will need to be reprofiled or replaced altogether.

Inspect the connecting rod bolts carefully for signs of stretching, (caused by overtightening), especially around where the threaded section ends. Replace them if you are in any doubt.

Bearing shells are quite easy to assess — if any of the copper backing is showing through they need replacing, although I always tend to fit replacement parts irrespective of their condition.

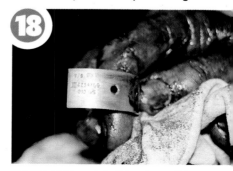

The size of all crankshaft bearings will be stamped on the back of the bearing shell. An engine fitted with undersize bearings has almost certainly been overhauled at least once before.

MGB GT

WORKSHOP RATING

TIME REQUIRED 6-8 hours

CCCCC

Part twenty: Peter Simpson begins engine reassembly.

Norman Hatcher popping number one piston into our MGB's rebored block. Fitting pistons isn't as easy as people imagine. Our picture sequence explains how it should be done!

LAST TIME, we left our MGB project's engine dismantled, with worn parts awaiting dispatch to MGB Hive's engine reconditioners. With the reconditioned and remade bits back from the machine shop we now start reassembly — building the bottom end up to and including fitting the oil sump.

Although fairly straightforward technically, this part of the job has to be done correctly because how well it's bolted together will have a crucial effect on how long the engine lasts. Experience has shown that when a rebuilt engine fails prematurely, the cause is nearly always duff assembly work.

It's particularly important to check the crank still turns freely after each operation. Turn it through one revolution, feeling for tight spots. Once you start fitting the pistons the action will tighten up significantly, and you may also feel slight changes in stiffness as the pistons go up and down, but overall the resistance should be even as the crank is turned. By turning after each and every operation you

will notice if the crank's action does suddenly become tighter, suggesting the problem must have been caused by whatever you did last.

Be fussy about clearances between moving components too. Pictures seven and ten show how to check crankshaft end-float using a dial gauge. This is the professional and accurate way of doing it, but if, like most of us, you don't have one of these useful tools, there's an alternative method using feeler gauges. With the centre bearing cap and all four thrust washers

in place, measure clearance between centre main bearing and thrust washers. It should be 0.051-0.076mm (0.002-0.003in).

You also need to check running clearances between bearings and the crankshaft. Norman, MGB Beehive's resident engine expert, does this using Plastigauge. Place a Plastigauge on the bearing, tighten the cap to the measured torque, and the width that the gauge has spread tells you the clearance. Simple! Unfortunately, Plastigauges are only available

B-SERIES ENGINE REASSEMBLY

1 First, ensure oilways and other drillings are totally free of dirt. This is important even if the cylinder block has just been cleaned chemically, as it's easy for dirt or dust to fall in during transport or storage.

2 The two brass plugs at each end of the engine should be removed when the block is chemically cleaned. They can't be reused, so after checking the oilways are clean you need to tap in new ones.

3 First of the new bearing shells to fit are the five main bearings mounted in the block. Make sure the metal behind is totally clear of dirt and muck, and the bearing shells should snap straight into place. The bearing running surface must be spotlessly clean too.

7 Now check the crankshaft end-float for the first time. It should be 0.051-0.076mm (0.002-0.003in). If you don't have a dial gauge see main text for an alternative method using feeler gauges.

8 Plastigauge in action. Place one of the gauge sections on the highest point of the crank journal like this. Then temporarily refit the relevant bearing cap and tighten to the specified torque setting.

9 Remove cap and measure the gauge's spread using the template. Our centre bearing's clearance was 0.038mm (0.0015in). That's within limits as it's meant to be 0.025-0.069mm (0.001-0.0027in).

in boxes of 100 but at £17.60 a box they're hardly expensive. For more details call Plastigauge on 01243 263613.

You may have noticed that our pistons came with conrods already attached. That's because on most MGB engines the gudgeon pins are a push-fit and have to be pressed into the pistons using a press. Most specialists will do this cheaply (some, including the MGB Hive, include it free) when you buy a rebored block and pistons. I reckon it's a good idea to obtain pistons and reboring services from the same supplier anyway — then you're not responsible for any problems with incompatibility.

Early engines, however, had a fully-floating gudgeon pin running in a brass bush in the conrod. These can be identified by having a circlip in the piston at each end of the gudgeon pin. This type won't need assembling in a press as the pin can be pushed out once the circlips are removed. Make sure you fit the conrods the right way round though. Most are marked 'front'; if not fit them so that the oil spray hole in the rod side faces the offside of the engine.

It's important to lubricate all moving surfaces as the engine is built up. This prevents corrosion on the machined surface and provides lubrication for the moving parts when the engine's started up for the first time. Without this, the bearings will run dry until oil has travelled round from the sump.

You can use ordinary engine oil if the unit's likely to be run fairly soon, say within six weeks of being built. However, if the engine is left longer, use special engine-building lubricant instead. Penrite list Engine Assembly Lube,

The MGB HIVE

THE project car featured on these pages belongs to and is being restored by the MGB Hive of Parsons Drove, Cambs. The MG will be for sale when work is completed.

If you are interested in buying the car, or just want to see how work is progressing, contact MGB Hive proprietor Nigel Petch (01945 700500). He says that *Practical Classics* readers are always welcome to the workshop.

As well as being the region's leading supplier of MGB parts, the company undertakes servicing and repairs along with restoration work at their Fenland premises near Wisbech.

TOOLS REQUIRED

- Torque wrench (see test in Dec 95 issue)
- Piston ring compressor
- Hammer with stout wooden shaft

TORQUE SETTINGS

- Big end bolts 4.8-5.5kg/m (35-40lb ft)
- Main bearings 9.7kg/m (70lb ft)
- Sump bolts 0.8kg/m (6lb ft)

which is available from any Penrite-appointed dealer in 40g containers. For details of stockists call Penrite on 0121 333 5237.

Next time we'll complete assembly of the short block, and cover setting the ignition and valve timing. We'll also be showing you the right way to do one job which several workshop manuals cover incorrectly.

USEFUL BACK ISSUES

Copies of these magazines are available from our Back Issues department, details on page 3.

Next, lubricate the bearing surfaces thoroughly. Use engine oil if the unit's going to be used within four to six weeks of rebuild, otherwise use special engine assembly lubricant instead (see text).

Before installing the crank, ensure the ground journals and internal oilways are all spotlessly clean, then lubricate as in step four. Once it's in, check crank turns freely and smoothly without binding.

Thrust washers each side of centre main bearing control end-float. Fit with cutouts facing outwards. Place in position, then slide round 180 degrees so they sit between block web and crankshaft.

After refitting and torquing cap again, recheck end-float, this time by levering between crank and centre bearing. Check end-float right round crank's circumference, and that crank turns freely.

Refit and check clearances of the bearings and bearing caps of numbers two and four main bearings. Caps are numbered and must be fitted in correct order and right way round. Then fit last two caps.

After each cap is fitted recheck end-float and that crank still turns freely without tight spots. Use airpower if you have it, but finally tighten bolts to correct setting using a good torque wrench.

NEXT ISSUE
REASSEMBLY CONTINUES

B-SERIES ENGINE REASSEMBLY

13 Being later-type conrods, ours came back from the reconditioner with the pistons already fitted. Ensure ring gaps are evenly spread around the piston's circumference before fitting piston in block.

14 Next, install big-end bearing shell into the conrod — again making sure backing surface is clean first, otherwise the shell will not sit properly. Oil the shell surface, but watch out for any particles of dirt.

15 Set crankshaft journal of piston to bottom dead centre. Then, after oiling bore, carefully insert the piston until the first (oil-control) ring is reached. Ensure pistons are installed the right way round.

16 Now take a piston ring compressor (these are cheap enough these days), tighten it around the piston so that rings are same diameter as piston, and tap the piston down using a wooden hammer shaft.

17 While doing this you must guide the other end using your other hand, to ensure conrod bolt ends don't foul and damage the crankshaft. Go gently, it's all too easy to damage the crank at this stage.

18 Then fit the other big-end bearing shell to the conrod cap and secure. Original nuts and bolts can be reused if undamaged, but if in doubt change them. Torque up to correct setting (see panel on p29).

19 With pistons installed, it's time to fit the camshaft. If using a new or reprofiled cam you'll need to transfer the woodruff key that fixes the timing sprocket's position. Tap key out using a chisel.

20 Lubricate mating surfaces of the cam, the bearing surfaces, camshaft lobes, and the oil pump/distributor drive teeth. Use storage oil if the engine's likely to be out of use for more than four to six weeks.

21 After lubricating the bearing surfaces inside the block, carefully slide the camshaft into place. Support the shaft's front inside the block, to prevent cam lobes from damaging bearing surfaces.

22 Oil pump goes on next. First replace pump studs if they were taken out while the block was away being machined. Then, after ensuring the mating surface is clean, fit paper gasket over the studs.

23 Then fit oil pump, using new shakeproof washers. Prime pump with oil (or storage lubricant) before fitting. It is wise to change oil pump irrespective of condition — a failed one can do immense damage.

24 Fit short lengths of cork into cutouts on front and rear main bearing caps. Use thin bead of instant gasket to keep sump gasket in place, then fit sump and tighten bolts in sequence a little at a time.

WORKSHOP RATING

TIME REQUIRED
6-8 hours

MGB GT

Part twenty-one: Peter Simpson completes our project MGB's B-series engine rebuild.

THIS ISSUE sees the installation of the timing gear plus fitting the cylinder head and associated parts. The work is slightly less critical in terms of clearances and working tolerances than the bottom-end buildup, but has to be carried out correctly if the engine is to give good service and remain oiltight. Oiltight? Yes, even BMC B-series engines can be leak-free for a while if they're assembled properly.

B-SERIES ENGINE REASSEMBLY

1 With the crank and camshafts installed, the next job is to fit the front plate. There's a gasket between this and the block, and a little instant gasket around outside the bolt holes will help keep things oiltight.

2 Next the plate itself is fitted — it can only go on one way. Make sure mating surface is scrupulously clean first. Note that the bolt holes double as fixings for other components so don't bolt plate down yet...

3 ...apart, that is, from in the centre where the camshaft retaining ring is attached by three ⁷⁄₁₆in A bolts passing through into the block. The old bolts can be reused here, but fit new sprung washers.

6 Timing chain tensioner goes on next. If the body bore has less than 0.076mm (0.003in) ovality, you can replace the plunger, but complete units only costs £6.50. Don't forget gasket and star washers.

7 Fit tensioner with plunger assembly retracted. To tension chain insert small drill bit into end and flick off locking tab. Check that timing marks still align once chain is tensioned (see picture 4).

8 Some workshop manuals tell you to install the distributor drive with valve timing marks aligned Wrong. The camshaft mark has to be exactly 180 degrees AWAY from direct alignment.

11 Refit cylinder head studs, remembering four longer studs go into holes adjacent to pushrod apertures to accommodate rocker gear. If you haven't a stud tool, screw in using the two nuts locked together technique.

12 Head gasket goes on next. Gasket is marked 'top' so be sure to fit correctly. Opinions on use of Instant Gasket on heads vary — some say it helps ensure a gas-tight seal, others that it shouldn't be necessary.

13 After fitting head, replace the shims, one of which sits under each rocker shaft pedestal. These often disappear from MGB engines over the years due to careless servicing. They should all have them.

MGB HIVE

THE project car featured on these pages belongs to and is being restored by the MGB Hive of Parsons Drove, Cambs. The MG will be for sale when work is completed.

If you are interested in buying the car, or just want to see how work is progressing, contact MGB Hive proprietor Nigel Petch (01945 700500). He says that *Practical Classics* readers are always welcome to the workshop.

As well as being the region's leading supplier of MGB parts, the company undertakes servicing and repairs along with restoration work at their Fenland premises near Wisbech.

Essentially it's all straightforward follow-the-picture-sequence stuff, with just a few points needing further clarification. There have,

however, been various minor internal changes to MGB engines over the years, and while our instructions are right for this 1971 car, there are a few detail differences which might affect pre-1966 and post-1977 cars in particular. For example, the distributor shaft setting procedure is different for post-1978 vehicles and some engines have a double timing chain with a different tensioner arrangement. Valve clearance settings also vary. It's essential, therefore, that this feature is used in conjunction with a good workshop manual — although as you'll see from the picture sequence, there's one part of this issue's work which some manuals don't get quite right.

The timing chain is something of a weak spot on the B-series engine. It tends to get noisy quite early on, although a noisy one may well carry on like it for years.

Nevertheless, we recommend fitting a new one virtually irrespective of condition. At £5.50 or £6.95 (depending whether it's a single or double chain), it's hardly worth even cleaning up the old one.

TIMING GEARS

THE CHAIN sprockets can be reused if unworn, and are quite easy to check. Look at the teeth shape. If they're symmetrical and the same shape all round the cog, it can be reused. If some or all of the teeth are hook-shaped the gear will need replacing.

Installing the head studs can be a bit tricky if you don't have a stud fitting tool. Don't try twisting them in using molegrips or similar. These will mark and thus weaken the studs, which isn't a good idea on components that have to be torqued down. The 'two nut' technique is much better. It works thus: take two cylinder head nuts and screw them both onto the stud so they touch. Fit the stud hand-tight first, then tighten the two nuts until they're hard up against each other. Then turn the top nut alone, and the stud should twist down into its hole. Remove the nuts by holding a spanner on the lower one while you undo the top. MGB studs are susceptible to corrosion, and a rusty stud should never be reused.

I haven't covered fitting valves to the head. You'd normally do this yourself when doing a top end overhaul at home, but a full engine

When fitting the timing chain set crank and cam so that when cam sprocket wheel is fitted the two punch-marks align. Then remove cam wheel, slip chain over both and install so the marks still align.

Once the chain is fitted and positioned correctly, fit nut and new tab washer, torque to 60-70lb ft, and knock tab washer over like this to lock nut in position. Nut requires 33mm (1¼in **AF**) socket.

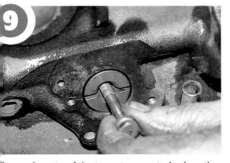

Then, using one of the tappet cover studs, drop the distributor driveshaft down into its hole with the offset slots running exactly straight across like this, and the larger of the half-moon sections on top.

As the driveshaft meshes, the action of the gear will make it turn until it ends up in roughly this position. Then fit retaining ring/collar on top (which may be a tight fit in 'hole') and hold down using setscrew.

Now install cam followers. Cover first with engine oil or assembly lubricant if engine will be unused for while. With new/reprofiled cam, these should be new. If not, refit in same hole that they came from.

Pushrods should, ideally, be refitted in the same positions too, but if the cam followers and/or rocker gear have been renewed it is less important. Make sure they drop right down into the cam followers.

USEFUL BACK ISSUES

Copies of these magazines are available from our Back Issues department, details on page 3.

B-SERIES ENGINE REASSEMBLY

Our rocker shaft was renewed and the rockers themselves reprofiled. Build the assembly up on the new shaft, making sure it all goes on in the correct order (see text). Use new split-pins to hold it all on.

Once rocker gear is built up it can be dropped into place on studs. Ensure pushrod ends sit inside adjuster screws as it goes down. Then tighten down using rocker nuts (not combined head/rocker nuts).

This rectangular pin often goes missing from MGBs. It is there to stop the rocker shaft from turning with the rocker action — taking the oilways out of line. It's held in position by this locking tab.

Torque head bolts in correct sequence (see manual) to 45-50lb ft, then set valve clearances to 0.38mm (0.015in) for inlet and exhaust, using the rule of nine (1 down, adjust 8 and so on). Recheck after 500 miles.

Norman usually leaves fitting the cam cover until almost last — on a bench it's easier to turn the engine with it off. The crank pulley aperture oil seal should be replaced as a matter of course.

Before fitting cam cover, pop oil thrower disc over end of crank. This spins loose on crank end to stop oil getting out. Fit with the F mark facing forwards. Different types of thrower are not interchangeable.

Now push the cam cover over the end, fit retaining bolts and washers, fingertight only until the external crank pulley is on. This will make it easier to fit the oil seal around the pulley, which is a tight fit.

This is the oil return outlet which is normally removed to facilitate block cleaning. Use new copper sealing washer on reassembly — an oil leak from here will cover your engine bay in minutes.

The oil pressure relief valve has been the cause of many unnecessary MGB engine rebuilds. If it sticks open the oil pressure will drop. As such, a new one (£4.25) was fitted, with new sealing washer.

---

overhaul is almost always accompanied by valve seat refacing or recutting. These days, it's also quite likely that hardened valve seats will be fitted to take unleaded petrol. Either way, the head will normally be supplied assembled and ready to fit with all the valves fully ground in. If not — follow the grinding in procedure in a manual.

ROCKER GEAR

THIS isn't normally overhauled except when an engine is being rebuilt — it gets noisy with age, but most people live with that. The rebuild process may, therefore, be unfamiliar. To dismantle, simply remove the split-pin from one end and take everything off. I advise laying out the various bits in the order that they come off to ease reassembly.

Usually, the rocker shaft itself is replaced

and if replacement rockers aren't available the existing ones are reprofiled. This process involves building up and polishing worn heels (the bit that contacts the valve), fitting new adjusting screws and drilling out the main centre hole to take a sleeve.

When building up the assembly, the basic order between each of the four pedestals is rocker-spring-rocker. On each outer edge though, one rocker sits outside each outermost pedestal, and is separated from the split-pin at each end of the shaft (which should, of course, be new) by a washer. Note too that the rocker shaft's position is fixed by a pin (picture 18) to prevent it from turning in service.

Alternatively, if you don't fancy doing all that, you can buy a complete exchange rocker gear. The MGB Hive do these for £42.50

TOOLS REQUIRED

- Torque wrench, screwdriver, feeler gauges
- 7/16, 1/2 and 9/16in AF spanners
- 1/2, 9/16 and 1 1/4in AF sockets
- Valve grinding sucker and paste

including VAT. Worth thinking about, given that a shaft alone costs £18.

That's the engine finished. In the Spring issue we'll move on to the gearbox and overdrive. While the overdrive is a tricky prospect for the DIY enthusiasts, there's no reason why you shouldn't tackle the gearbox yourself.

NEXT ISSUE
Gearbox and overdrive

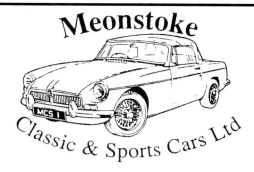

WORKSHOP RATING

TIME REQUIRED
3 hours

C C C C

MGB GT

Part twenty two: Peter Simpson explains how to take an MGB gearbox apart. That's the easy bit!

ALTHOUGH stripping a gearbox is easy, it shouldn't be rushed. It's especially important that you work systematically and store the parts methodically — but more of that in a moment.

BASIC PRINCIPLES

GEARBOXES may look complicated, but most found on classic cars are straightforward designs and are simple to overhaul, provided you understand the basic principles and have enough mechanical sympathy to assess what's worn and what isn't.

An MGB gearbox basically works thus: there's a mainshaft running from one end to the other. This is split in two inside the 'box so the front and back sections can spin independently of each other. The front part is called the input or first motion shaft, the back the output or third motion shaft.

Alongside this there is a layshaft with a one-piece cluster of five cogs on it. The shaft itself is fixed in position but the gear cluster

is free to spin independently of it. The front gear on the layshaft is meshed permanently with one on the gearbox input shaft, but at the back, drive is selected by moving the appropriate gear in and out of mesh with one on the layshaft by sliding it up and down the mainshaft. Each speed normally has its own cog on both the main and lay shafts and the box is set up so that only one pair of gears is connected at any one time.

Once, gears slid directly on the shaft by means of splines, which stopped them from turning independently of it, but on most modern boxes this action is controlled by synchromesh rings and couplings. When the change is made the synchromesh hub is activated before a gear is engaged and this synchronises the speeds at which the layshaft and mainshaft are turning before the gear goes in, thus giving a smooth, clean action.

The gears are moved about by operating forks which are connected to the gearlever via rods, and act on the synchromesh assem-

blies. To prevent the gears from jumping out once selected, the selector rods incorporate spring-loaded balls. When a gear is selected these are pushed down into a matching aperture in the casing. This gives enough resistance to stop the gear from jumping out on its own, but the spring's resistance is easily overcome when the gearlever is operated.

Ball-locking systems are also often used as part of the mechanism to prevent more than one gear being selected at once. Most gearboxes found in classics, including the MGB, have three selector forks and rods — one for first and second, one for third and fourth and

GEARBOX STRIPDOWN

1 First drain the oil. Do this even if the gearbox was drained *in situ* before removal because this doesn't usually get it all out. By lifting each end of the 'box in turn you can now get most of the oil out.

2 Remove this side cover (ten ½in AF bolts) so you can inspect the innards and decide whether an overhaul is viable. Check for wear as explained in text. Note configuration of bolts, screw-heads and washers.

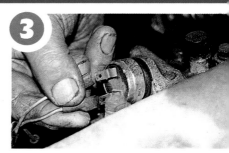

3 Before removing remote control extension from 'box you will need to disconnect the leads from the overdrive inhibitor switch, which prevents overdrive being engaged in first, second or reverse.

7 A thin spacing washer behind the cover often remains stuck in position. The shaft with the semi-circular cutout section just above Norman's fingers is the layshaft, which the cover helps lock in place.

8 Next, take the overdrive unit off. Undo the eight ⁷⁄₁₆in AF nuts holding the unit on. Then use a strong screwdriver to push the unit back by its stud, and pull it off the end. Expect some oil seepage.

9 Overdrive unit is powered by this cam mounted on the output shaft. As it slides off, be ready to catch the ball bearing which locks its position on the shaft. Then take off the circlip in front of it.

_T: the MGB Hive's Norman Hatcher isn't just an _ine man — he's pretty good at overhauling _rboxes too. Here he's removing the lever remote _using from off our B-series engine gearbox._

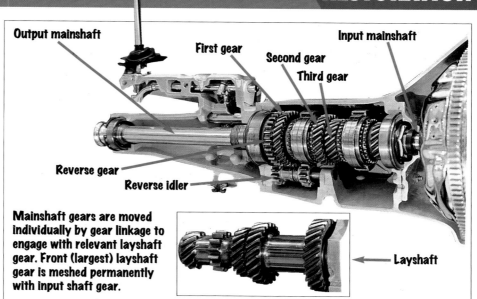

Output mainshaft

Input mainshaft

First gear

Second gear

Third gear

Reverse gear

Reverse idler

Mainshaft gears are moved individually by gear linkage to engage with relevant layshaft gear. Front (largest) layshaft gear is meshed permanently with input shaft gear.

Layshaft

e for reverse, but some manage with fewer _ds, though separate forks are still required.
Gears are used only for first, second and third gear.
Fourth is normally a straight 1:1 ratio achieved by linking the input and output shafts directly — the layshaft isn't involved.
Although gear-wheels always reverse the direction of drive, drive comes out of the 'box in the same direc-tion as it went in because it goes through two sets of cogs — one going on to the layshaft, _ other coming off. For reverse the direc-_n needs to be changed. This is achieved by _erting an additional set of gears between _ layshaft and third motion shaft. This is _ reverse idler and, like the layshaft, the _ster turns on a stationary shaft.

ISMANTLING TIPS

_KING any gearbox apart is one of those _s that leaves you knee-high in screws, _ings, ball-bearings and the like, many of _ich are tiny, look similar to each other _t usually aren't) and are easily lost. Some _hese parts are non-wearing too, making

TOOLS REQUIRED

● ⁷⁄₁₆in, ½in and ⁹⁄₁₆in AF spanners or sockets.
● Engineering hammer, circlip pliers (external) and a stout brass drift.

replacements hard to find.
Keep sub-assemblies as built-up as possi-ble after removing to help you to determine what goes where during the rebuild.
Bear in mind, too, that reconditioned gear-boxes are readily available for these cars for around £250. That is probably cheaper than overhauling a 'box needing a lot of work.

The MGB HIVE

THE project car featured on these pages belongs to and is being restored by the MGB Hive of Parsons Drove, Cambs. The MG will be for sale when work is completed.
If you are interested in buying the car, or just want to see how work is progressing, contact MGB Hive proprietor Nigel Petch (01945 700500). He says that _Practical Classics_ readers are always welcome to the workshop.
As well as being the region's leading supplier of MGB parts, the company undertakes servicing and repairs along with restoration work at their Fenland premises near Wisbech.

4 _er undoing the four ½in AF bolts holding exten-_ housing down, tap under the back end with a _ss drift to remove. Non-overdrive gearboxes _e a tower here, but removal is the same.

5 Then put a screwdriver underneath the top of the interlock plate and bracket assembly (which sits on a flange horizontally just inside the housing), and carefully tease it out from the casing.

6 Turning now to the front of the 'box, the next job is to remove the front bearing cover assembly (which incorporates the clutch operating arm pivot). There are seven ½in AF nuts this time.

0 _w it's time to detach the back (extension) _ing from the main part of the gearbox. Undo _ five bolts and three securing nuts, taking care _ retrieve the spring washers behind them.

11 Push back the selector lever that's accessible through the gearlever/extension aperture on top, and carefully pull the housing off the back, supporting the weight of the casting as you go.

12 Start dismantling main gearbox assembly by undoing the lock-nut securing the first/second and third/fourth selector forks. Sometimes the bolts are locked with wire as an additional precaution.

You can get a good idea of what's likely to be involved by simply undoing the side cover (picture 1) and turning the shafts. Inspect the gear teeth carefully. If any are chipped or severely worn, an exchange unit will probably be more cost-effective than doing an overhaul yourself. If the main gear cluster is damaged, it will almost certainly have damaged the laygear it meshes with unless the fault occurred suddenly and the car was taken off the road for immediate repairs.

If you do decide to replace gears, it's not usually a good idea to fit new ones in isolation. Meshing a sharp, tight new cog with a part-worn (but still perfectly serviceable) used one often causes noisy operation and quicker wear of the old one. Far better to obtain a good secondhand one in similar condition to the rest of the gearbox.

Wear is relatively uncommon on these gearboxes. But when it does occur, the cause is usually either bad driving or a gearbox being run over a long period with insufficient oil and/or worn bearings. The latter will allow excess sideways movement of the shafts and cause rapid wear.

We're not covering overdrive overhaul because it's not something we recommend that you do yourself. Exchange units cost around £175 from MGB specialists such as MGB Hive.

The gearbox shown in the picture sequence is the all-synchro (1967-on) overdrive unit from our 1971 GT. Earlier and/or non-overdrive boxes differ slightly but, as far as dismantling procedures are concerned, they are virtually identical. Next time, we'll see what needs replacing or refurbishing and what doesn't, and start putting it all back together. Which, as I said earlier, is the skilled bit...

GEARBOX STRIPDOWN

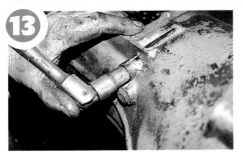

Then undo the three bolts at the front of the housing to release the detent springs and plungers. Careful — they are trapped in there under tension and tend to pop out unexpectedly.

Using a soft brass drift or similar, carefully tap out the two selector shafts. Don't take the levers off the end — these are used to knock against. Retrieve each selector fork as it falls free of its shaft.

Next remove the reverse gear idler. First, knock the locking tab back. Then undo and withdraw the bolt and tap the shaft out. This will release the idler gear cluster which can then be extracted from the back.

Now withdraw the layshaft. Push it through from the back using a dowel smaller than the shaft so that the gear cluster and its thrust washers are retained but able to fall away from the mainshaft.

Using a suitable brass drift on the mainshaft first gear (the biggest one) and a fairly heavy hammer, knock the third motion shaft out through the back. Make sure that the laygear is out of the way first.

Eventually the shaft will come out and away, complete with its back bearing and housing. Pull the complete assembly out and away but don't dismantle it yet — that's for the next issue.

Retrieve third and fourth synchro hubs. Invert casing on two pieces of wood about 5cm (2in) thick and, after again ensuring the laygear is clear, knock input shaft and bearing out.

Finally, take out dowel complete with laygear and thrust washers. Now give everything a thorough cleaning/degreasing. We'll cover stripping the input and output shafts, and assessing wear next time.

USEFUL BACK ISSUES

Copies of these magazines are available from our Back Issues department, details on page 3.

NEXT ISSUE
Gearbox and overdrive

WORKSHOP RATING

TIME REQUIRED
6–8 hours (including cleaning)

C C C C C

MGB GT

Part twenty three: Peter Simpson shows how our MGB's gearbox internals were checked for wear and reports on the reassembly procedure.

LAST TIME, we left the gearbox broken down into its main component parts. It's now time to strip and rebuild the first and third motion shaft assemblies, and refit these into the box. This is covered by the picture sequence. But first, here are a few tips on checking gearbox components for wear and deciding whether or not to replace them.

The first bit is easy — all needle and roller bearings, oil seals and gaskets should be renewed irrespective of condition. Bearings are the most wear-prone parts of any gearbox, but they're relatively inexpensive and having come this far, it would be a false economy to reuse any of them.

Moving on to the gears, problems like chipped or broken teeth aren't uncommon, especially if the box was particularly noisy in one gear. Damage like this is obvious but if you find a missing or badly broken tooth

check the mating gear for damage, too.

Check also that the teeth are the same shape and the edges are formed correctly. There should be a small machined 45 degree chamfer on each edge. The gears should be a matt silver colour as shown in the pictures. A light straw colouring inside the teeth, or an overall black colour mean they've overheated due to oil starvation. It takes a lot to do this to an MGB box, but gearbox oil level is sometimes forgotten during servicing. Check for a damaged casing too if you find this.

Normally the small dog teeth around the outside of each gear wear first — they're the ones which mesh with the synchromesh hub when changing gear. The edges should all be a consistent, clean, rounded shape. Light burring can sometimes be removed by careful grinding (see picture 9), but severe chewing means that the cluster needs replacing.

Spline edges on gears and shafts should be straight and the splines themselves of even height all along, except for any machined taper at the ends. Check too for wear lines shafts around the outside, where gears have sat. Light circumference lines are common and can be cleaned off, but wear felt when

GEARBOX REBUILD

1 Strip input shaft first — it's more straightforward. Undo nut (left-hand thread and there's a locktab) in front of main bearing. As you can see, an old clutch plate is ideal for holding the shaft stationary.

2 Drive shaft out of input bearing (which should always be renewed) by hitting end with a copper-headed mallet. A scrap MGB engine block bore is the right size to support bearing — but use a scrap block.

3 Support third motion shaft assembly in a vice, using a block of wood to take shaft's weight. Vice jaws should grip splined end section of shaft only, and use soft jaw protectors to prevent any damage.

6 Undo the locknut halfway down the shaft and remove the speedo drive pinion. You can knock the shaft out of the remaining bearing and first and reverse gears. As you can see, an old starter motor body is exactly the right size to support the bearing.

7 This is the small spigot bearing that sits between the first and third motion shafts and allows them to turn independently. Shaft pitting (which is too bad to grind out) was caused by a badly worn bearing.

8 Checking synchro hubs for wear. Ensure outer and inner slide freely and look for damage at spline end. The two synchro hubs (the third-fourth one slides off shaft when it's removed) aren't interchangeable.

OOLS REQUIRED

- Copper-headed mallet
- Engineering hammer, punch
- Length of tube 2.5cm (1in) diameter
- Good feeler gauges
- Screwdriver, large adjustable spanner

FT: The MGB Hive's Norman Hatcher installing the rd motion shaft. Care is needed to guide it into e first motion shaft's spigot bearing hole.

nning a finger over the mark may be more rious and should be checked by an expert.
Check the bearing seatings too — especially r roller bearings. Again, light marking can ground out, but anything more severe eans the shaft probably needs changing. afts occasionally bend or run out of true heck by rolling across a flat surface) though is normally only happens following seizure. eck shafts too for black overheating marks, hich can often be polished out.
Similar checks apply to the synchromesh bs. Make sure the two parts slide evenly d that there's no more than very slight ovement when the inner and outer are isted against each other.
Try the hub on its shaft, checking that it des up and down freely. Again, light dam- e to the hub spline ends (making the action ght) can often be removed by careful use of grinding disc, as shown. But remember, you n't eliminate wear this way.
I'd always replace any gears, shafts or syn- romesh hubs that need renewing with good condhand ones. Apart from the cost and ailability advantages (if you can't get

individual parts you can always buy a complete box and build a good one from the two) a secondhand replacement is likely to work better with the rest of the box. Think about it. Which will be kinder to the existing gears, a new cog with sharp teeth or one that's done a similar mileage to those it's meshing with?

BUILDING IT UP

EVERYTHING that goes back into the box must be scrupulously clean. Even one tiny spec of grit or dirt in the wrong place can wreak havoc. Half-cleaning is often worse than doing nothing, because you'll dislodge dirt which was previously stuck out of harm's way. So make sure you clean everything properly as you go, and if you're rebuilding the box some time after the main clean, do it again. Give particular attention to the casing innards and all the splines, and if any machining has been done, check there's no swarf left. A good machine shop should do this as a matter of course, but it does no harm to check.

SETTING ENDFLOAT

GEARBOX components have to be assembled and installed to achieve exactly the right amount of resistance before a turning component starts to move, and so that there's a set amount of sideways movement on a shaft between certain gears and other components. If these settings are wrong the box will have a shorter life and will probably be noisy. We'll cover setting the turning resistance (or pre-load) next time — it's quite easy on an MGB.
However, the sliding movement or endfloat is checked when the third motion shaft's built up and, in the layshaft's case, when that's

The MGB HIVE

THE project MGB GT car featured on these pages is being restored by the MGB Hive of Parsons Drove, Cambridgeshire (01945 700500).
An enthusiast has recently agreed to buy the car when work is complete. But if you want to see how things are progressing, contact MGB Hive proprietor Nigel Petch. He says that *Practical Classics* readers are always welcome.
As well as being the region's leading supplier of MGB parts, the company undertakes servicing and repairs along with restoration work at their Fenland premises near Wisbech.

fitted. This is another job that frightens many people off gearbox overhaul, but it's quite straightforward. Once the shaft's built up, but before bending the locking tab(s) over (so you can dismantle it again if necessary), insert an appropriate-sized feeler gauge between the gear being checked and whatever is next to it (the casing mating surface in the laygear's case). Our table gives the settings.
Endfloat is varied by changing the thrust washer thickness. The manuals say to do this by substituting thicker or thinner washers. In practice, though, it's often hard to obtain the complete range of thicknesses these days, so most reconditioners (including the MGB Hive) just grind a thicker thrust washer down to suit. You can do this too, as long as you can grind the surface totally flat. The endfloat is usually within limits anyway unless major components have been changed.
Finally, the box shown here is the four-synchromesh unit fitted as standard from October 1967 and since retro-fitted to many ▶

USEFUL BACK ISSUES

Copies of these magazines are available from our Back Issues department, details on page 3.

art taking shaft apart by knocking back front lock- asher's locktab. Then undo washer. Use a C span- r if you have one, otherwise knock it off carefully ing a drift inside holes. Don't burr the outside.

Side off third and second gears and thrust washers (one between the two, and one between second gear and synchrohub). Then remove hub. See text for how to check for gear wear and damage.

you're careful you can eliminate light burring to eth ends using a soft (paper backed) grinding sc. It's not particularly easy and unless you're ery competent it might be best left to a specialist.

Building up first and third motion shafts is a reversal of dismantling. Here reverse gear is being refitted to mainshaft. Lube between all moving surfaces to ensure they're protected when the box is first used.

earlier cars. This is the most common MGB box. The earlier three-synchro units, although similar have important differences. The third motion stripdown and rebuild is more involved. Some parts are scarce, too. If you're planning to overhaul one of these a thorough reading of the manual beforehand is essential. I'd also check out parts availability.

Even if you're tackling a four-synchro box you should use these instructions in conjunction with a good workshop manual. We cannot cover every possibility, or even every stage of the job. As always, our aim is to supplement the manual, and pass on dodges used by the professionals.

NEXT ISSUE: finishing gearbox rebuild

GEARBOX REBUILD

When refitting thrust washers make sure lugs on next gear sit in cut-outs. Before bending locktabs check first, second and third gear endfloats: 0.13-0.2mm (0.005-0.008in) with feeler gauge between gears.

Laygear assembly's a one-piece casting but roller bearings inside should always be replaced. Two caged bearings separated by a distance piece should pull out easily. Oil cages then slide back in.

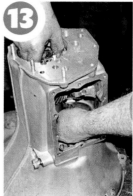

We can now start building up the box itself. First job is to place the laygear assembly (plus thrust washers) inside, but don't fit the layshaft yet. Instead, retain the assembly using a thinner dummy piece of rod (a spare pushrod's ideal) so it can move sideways.

Laygear thrust washers have to be fitted so their locking tabs each fit into a moulding in body casting, to prevent them turning. This is the front washer — back one is similar but has two-pronged locking tab.

Next refit first motion shaft. Start it by tapping on the centre using a piece of tube that's sitting on the locking nut (not the bearing) as a drift. Once the bearing's inside the housing you can tap its outer edges (each side a little at a time) until it is fully home.

Third and fourth synchromesh assembly is loose on end of the third motion shaft so it's far easier to place the synchromesh hub inside first and then thread the shaft through as it goes down and in.

Install third motion assembly as shown in heading shot. Make sure dowel in body casting lines up with cut-out in bearing outer — this is a locking device to prevent the bearing from turning inside the body.

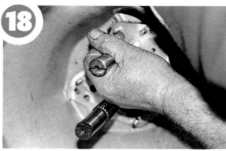

Now fit layshaft. Oil then press it in from front by hand, pushing the dummy shaft out as you go. Don't dislodge thrust washers. It must end up with raised D section on top — this is locked by front cover.

Check laygear endfloat with a screwdriver between casting and gear, and feel for side movement. Measure between one end and thrust washer with feeler gauge. It should be 0.05-0.08mm (0.002-0.003in).

Reverse idler sits at back of box and spins on a stationary shaft via phosphor-bronze bushes. Bushes have to be pressed in and then reamed to size — a machine shop job. Oil bearing surfaces generously.

After placing gear cluster inside box, push shaft in from behind. Like layshaft this shouldn't be overtight — it should slide slightly stiffly down under modest screwdriver pressure in the slot at the back like this.

Watch for small hole as the shaft emerges. Align with threaded hole in casting by twisting as required. Screw shaft locking nut (remember lock washer) so end goes through to stop shaft from turning.

MGB GT

WORKSHOP RATING

TIME REQUIRED **4-5 hours**

C C C C C

Part twenty-four: Peter Simpson concludes the gearbox overhaul.

L AST TIME we completed assembly of the main gearbox internals, including the mainshaft, layshaft and reverse idler assemblies. As we saw then, none of this is really that difficult, but it does all have to be done correctly and with care if the completed box is to give good service long-term. All that remains is to install the operating rods and forks which push and pull the appropriate cogs into line when the gearlever is moved (via a remote control extension linkage in this case).

GEARING UP

THE FORKS sit around a collar on each cog which has to be moved to engage gear, and are connected via rods to the gearlever.

The rods incorporate stops to prevent more than one gear being selected at once and sprung plungers prevent the gear from coming out of mesh, while still allowing changes in gear to be made.

When the box is out of gear, the plunger presses against the side of the rod, and the rod is free to slide up and down. However, when a gear is engaged the plunger falls into a small cut-out in the rod, thus locking it into position. The plunger's resistance, although sufficient to stop the box from jumping out of gear, is easily overcome when the rod is moved by hand to change gear. Each rod has its own plunger and spring.

I expect that those of you whose gearboxes occasionally jump are already thinking that you could cure it by simply renewing those springs and plungers. It sometimes works, and if the plungers are easily accessible without dismantling the box, it's worth a try. On many boxes (including our four-synchro MGB unit) the detent springs and plungers are housed under external bolt

heads — some (not alas, the MGB's) can even be reached without taking the box off! However, worn rods and selector forks can also cause gear jumping so don't be too disappointed if changing the plungers and springs makes no difference whatsoever.

FRONT AND BACK

THE OTHER tasks to be tackled this time are fitting the box's front cover and, at the other end, the overdrive unit.

As the first few pictures show, fitting the front cover is quite critical. Although it's important to get the setting correct, doing so is not particularly difficult once you know how. Picture 2 shows the technique — we fitted the circlip last time, but it's easy enough to take it out again temporarily for this purpose. Although Norman used an input bearing

GEARBOX REBUILD

1 Front cover and clutch arm mount contains shims which effectively set the first motion shaft's endfloat. Two sizes of shim are available — **0.05mm (0.002in)** and **0.10mm (0.004in)**.

2 To set shaft's endfloat, fit sufficient shim(s) so that the box front bearing circlip is flush with the cover's machined surface plus its sealing gasket. Use a straight edge to check as shown here.

6 Thread the selector rods through from behind. Note that the 3rd/4th rod happens to pass through the 1st/2nd fork, though it isn't connected and operates totally independently of it.

7 Push rods in and turn them until the cut-out section is opposite the threaded bolt hole in its fork. Then fit locking bolts and, once they're screwed right in, tighten the locking nut down to lock it.

to hold the clip down this isn't really essential — anything that's the right size to hold the clip right down all round will do — even the old bearing if it came out in one piece!

Fitting the overdrive isn't that difficult either, as long as you know what to do. Getting it to slide properly over the gearbox output shaft can take a little fiddling (take care not to lose the overdrive unit's centralisation as you lift it off the bench) but if you go steady and take your time it'll slide down smoothly. It's a great help if the gearbox is set so that the overdrive oil pump operating cam (picture 14) is on the opposite side of the box to where the overdrive plunger will be once it's in place — but if not you can push the plunger back using a long screwdriver.

Obviously a little jiggling of the input shaft is needed to align the gearbox and overdrive splines. This isn't difficult if the splines are clean, but if you turn the overdrive internals while doing this take care ONLY to turn them in the normal direction of travel — anti-clockwise with the unit on the bench and its front facing you, or clockwise when it's being dropped on to the gearbox.

Don't bother trying to overhaul the overdrive unit yourself. Specialist equipment and knowledge are needed for that. You'd probably also have difficulty obtaining spare parts — hardly anyone stocks them because outside the specialist trade there isn't any demand. Many overdrive faults are actually caused by defective wiring, the solenoid, a blocked oil filter or low oil pressure. These

TOOLS REQUIRED

- **Good straight edge**
- **⅜, ⁷⁄₁₆ & ½AF spanner and sockets**
- **Long screwdriver**

are all common faults which can be fixed fairly easily, but leave anything else to the specialist. Good reconditioned units cost around £175 exchange.

The gearbox here is a four-synchro overdrive unit. Obviously there are differences between four and three-synchro units and between overdrive and non-overdrive boxes, though many principles are the same. In particular, the three-synchro boxes had an internal selector rod detent spring arrangement incorporating a block which houses all three plungers and through which the rods pass. This is rather more tricky to build up as you have to push each rod's spring and plunger in from on top and then hold them down with a screwdriver while you push the rod through both the plunger block and its fork. Not that difficult when it all goes well, but infuriating if the spring pings out — especially if it ends up inside the box.

The main difference between an overdrive and non-overdrive box is the tailpiece — it's longer on non-overdrive boxes. If you're tackling one of these do fit the propshaft bolts into the propshaft flange before fitting the flange to the back of the box. There isn't enough room to get them in with the flange ▶

...ice you know how many shims are required in ...e housing you can press in the front oil seal. ...is can be installed without a press, but only if ...u're careful. Lubricate it well with grease.

Then, with the gasket and shims in position, pop the front cover over and tighten the ½AF securing nuts down evenly to avoid damaging the gasket and ensure the preload remains correct.

It's now time to fit the selector forks. The 1st/2nd speed fork, shown here, goes on the back synchro hub, the 3rd/4th on the forward one, and the reverse selector sits on the reverse idler.

...w fit the detent plungers and springs — ...nger goes in first followed by spring. On four-...chro boxes all three go on the side like this. ...e third hole is behind the raised front one.

Take the rear extension piece, refit the selector lever if it's been removed (which isn't always necessary) and then check that it's free to move up, down and around the selector lever shaft.

Drop the complete assembly on to the main box assembly, not forgetting the gasket between them. Note that it's held down by a mixture of bolts and nuts on studs — all ½AF.

on the gearbox. This applies to the overdrive units too, but a good exchange unit will come with the flange (and bolts) already fitted.

Next issue our car makes a welcome reappearance. It now looks a wee bit different from when we last saw it, because while Norman's been overhauling the key mechanical components, Neil Fincham's renovated the shell. It's also been painted and it looks superb even before cutting and polishing. So we'll be starting the big buildup from bright red shell back into a fully functioning motor car.

GEARBOX REBUILD

Select fourth gear and fit the interlock arm assembly — this doesn't normally need to be dismantled. Fit it the correct way round so that its mounting plate matches cut-outs in extension top.

At this point **Norman** spotted a little very light burring on the mainshaft's end splines. However, it was easily removed using an air sander and disc. We advise wearing gloves when you do this.

Overdrive oil pump is driven off mainshaft by a cam held in position by a ball-bearing — or sometimes a woodruff key. First, fit the circlip underneath, then push the ball into its aperture like this.

Once you've done that, push the operating cam down onto the circlip. When in place the circlip will hold the ball-bearing in position, and the ball will fix the location of the cam on the shaft.

With the reconditioned overdrive unit unpacked, line up internal components by eye using a long screwdriver, so the overdrive will slip on. Take care to turn internal components anti-clockwise only.

The other way of aligning the overdrive is with an actual mainshaft — either a spare or the box's own before assembly. This pump plunger contacts the cam and may have to be pushed back like this.

Once overdrive is aligned correctly push it right down, but don't force it — if it doesn't go fairly easily find out why. Then fit the securing nuts, not forgetting the sprung washers underneath.

Almost there! Refit the side cover and gasket next, after taking a final look inside to make sure everything appears to be as it should. Ten ½AF bolts plus the inevitable star washers.

NEXT ISSUE: fitting up begins

Once the overdrive internals are lined up, slip the unit over the mainshaft. Do this with top gear engaged and jiggle the input until everything aligns. Screwdriver (bottom) is used to push pump plunger back.

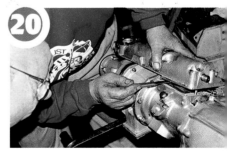

After checking that the remote housing is operating as it should place it in position, making sure the extension's linkage end fits into the box's. Then bolt it down — and that's it, one box rebu

CLASSIC EXAMPLES
OF HOW TO SAVE MONEY!

1956 • MORRIS MINOR • £55.63 !! Value £2,000

1965 • MGB ROADSTER • £76.13 !! Value £5,000

1976 • TRIUMPH SPITFIRE • £81.25 !! Value £3,500

1953 • AUSTIN HEALEY • £117.13 !! Value £15,000

1968 • JAGUAR 'E' TYPE • £153.00 !! Value £20,000

Above are typical examples of how much you can expect to pay for fully comprehensive insurance through Richardson Hosken Specialist Car Division. And the good news is that just because we are cheaper doesn't mean you lose out on service. **Now you can insure your Classic Car for less without reducing your cover.** With over 20 years experience in Classic, Vintage and Veteran Car Insurance we can provide unsurpassed cover at an unrivalled price.

Compare the benefits of your current cover with the benefits our customers enjoy :

- **The Most Competitive Fully Comprehensive premiums for policies up to 5,000 Miles**
- **Agreed Values at no extra cost**
- **Automatic Rally Cover (excluding racing, pacemaking and speed testing)**
- **Cover on dismantled parts**
- **Personal Accident Cover of up to £5,000 whilst travelling in any vehicle**
- **Easy pay Instalment scheme**
- **Return of Salvage Free of Charge (On all vehicles over 20 years old)**

Our quality of service speaks for itself, we are the official brokers for The **Rolls Royce** Enthusiasts Club, The **Stag Owners Club**, The **Bentley Drivers** Club, The **Austin Seven** Club, The **Historic Sports Car** Club, The **Austin Ten** Owners Club, and The **Classic and Sportscar** Club in addition to thousands of Individual Classic Car owners.

THE MOST COMPETITIVE CLASSIC CAR INSURANCE AVAILABLE FOR DRIVERS OVER 25 YEARS OLD

——— THAT'S OUR POLICY! ———
Ring 01277 206 911 NOW FOR AN IMMEDIATE QUOTE

OR SEND COMPLETED FORM OVERLEAF TO THE FREEPOST ADDRESS BELOW

Richardson Hosken Specialist Car Division
FREEPOST, Library House, New Road, Brentwood, Essex, CM14 4ZP
A member of the Coyle Hamilton Group of Companies

MGB GT

WORKSHOP RATING
TIME REQUIRED 6-8 hours
C C C C

Part twenty–five: the final reassembly begins!
Peter Simpson reports as our MGB shell
reappears and starts the long buildup back into
a fully-functioning motor car.

Welcome back Neil Fincham. A familiar face from the MGB Hive returns to our MGB project coverage for the shell reassembly and fitting-up stage.

AT LAST, after several issues renovating the engine and gearbox, our project MGB bodyshell has reappeared. And as you can see, it looks a lot better than when we saw it back in December 1995

Since then, the MGB Hive's Neil Fincham has replicated the repairs we saw being done on the nearside on the offside of the bodyshell. Once all the structural work was finished the car was wheeled round to the paintshop where the MGB Hive's other Neil prepared the shell and then applied the superb coat of two-pack it now wears.

We haven't covered the paintwork in detail because two-pack paint contains highly toxic isocynates and must be applied with proper equipment. This includes a full spraybooth with proper filtering arrangements and an air-fed mask (taking air from outside the operating area) for the operator. It also requires a different application technique from materials such as cellulose. And even if a DIY restorer can get access to the equipment, it's highly unlikely that anyone will sell you the materials.

TAKE YOUR TIME

FINAL assembly is the part of any project which can take an inordinately long time. However, it's certainly not something to rush

BODYSHELL BUILDUP

1

Painted shell was left on its running gear to improve manoeuvrability, and steering column and handbrake were masked rather than removed, although the column was lowered for painting the underdash.

2

New door hinges are strongly recommended — they make door alignment and adjustment easier and improve the car's general feel. Set doors initially so the swage line joins evenly at the front and back.

3

Make sure all screw holes are clear of paint before you start — don't rely on turning the bolts in to do this. If you don't have a tap and die set — any pointed instrument used carefully will do the job just as well.

7

Lift quarterlight glass and chrome surround up and out. Dump old rubber seal — they always leak after dismantling. Half-way pivot needs to come off; just undo the two screws holding it down and extract.

8

The old frame cleaned up remarkably well. Neil finds that it's easiest to start fitting the new quarterlight rubber at the top and then work down. Make sure it goes fully into its channel on both sides.

9

Here we're refitting the cleaned up quarterlight — it goes in from the outside. As you can see, our quarterlight pivot didn't snap off and was reused, although spring and securing nut were renewed.

because how well your car's bolted together will largely determine how good it looks. Sloppy assembly always shows up — remember BL in the late 1970s? — whereas a properly put together car should be indistinguishable from a vehicle that has been well put together at the factory.

Take particular care over things like panel fit, and make a point of using all the fixings that the manufacturer used. This includes all the spacers and lock washers. It's sometimes tempting to miss out the odd sprung washer, but things like this weren't normally fitted without a reason and a bolt fitted without its lock washer will work loose before too long.

To keep the reassembly coverage manageable, we'll be concentrating over the next few issues on those parts of the car which we haven't shown coming apart. That's because in virtually every case, reassembly is a straightforward reversal of dismantling.

RENEW OR REFURBISH? ■

AS YOU can buy more or less anything you want for an MGB it's tempting to renew everything in sight that isn't perfect. But, while individual parts aren't that expensive, the overall cost soon mounts up and it's easy to spend an absolute fortune without realising it. I know, I've been there and done it!

Obviously if you're planning to produce a perfect, concours-winning car then you'll want everything to be perfect and will probably accept that this quality won't come cheap. Let's face it though, many of us have

The MGB HIVE ■

THE project MGB GT car featured on these pages is being restored by the MGB Hive of Parsons Drove, Cambridgeshire (01945 700500).

An enthusiast from Holland has recently bought the car but if you want to see how they do things, contact MGB Hive proprietor Nigel Petch. He says that *Practical Classics* readers are always welcome.

As well as being the region's leading supplier of MGB parts, the company undertakes servicing and repairs along with restoration work at their Fenland premises near Wisbech.

to finance our hobbies from a very tight budget these days, and if you're after a good-looking usable car rather than a prize-winning example, you'll probably be happier spending less and refurbishing something that can be made nearly as good as new with a little elbow grease.

By seeing what's involved you can decide which course you want to follow. After all, removing and refitting something that's been refurbished is exactly the same as removing an old bit and fitting a new one.

If, like me, your classic interests are, shall we say, a little more obscure than MGBs, you won't have this problem. Lovers of old Hillmans don't normally have the luxury of lots of remanufactured parts to choose from. For us, if it's not still available as new, old stock there are two choices — refurbish what you've got or find a better secondhand bit and do that up!

(4) Door striker plate attaches via overlarge holes and separate threaded plates behind. The plates are free to move slightly all round, thus allowing the lock's (and thus the door's) position to be adjusted.

Original window surround assembly wasn't salvageable, so Neil found a better one in the MGB Hive's spares department. First job was to remove corner finishing plate. Watch out for rusted-up screws.

This pin and spring form quarterlight bottom pivots, the latter being held on by a locking nut. Chances are the pivot will snap as you undo the nut. Don't worry — it's a separate piece and only £2.95 new.

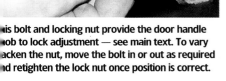

is bolt and locking nut provide the door handle ob to lock adjustment — see main text. To vary acken the nut, move the bolt in or out as required d retighten the lock nut once position is correct.

Handle is secured to door by two bolts from inside, but don't forget the fibre gasket under each contacting part of the door. Don't overtighten securing bolts — the threads in the handle might strip out.

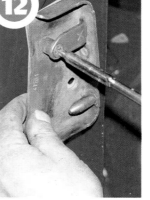

Next, Neil fitted the cleaned-up door striker plate. It's secured to the sliding back plates (see picture 4) by three cross-headed screws. Tighten so plate can slide slightly stiffly for now.

TROUBLE IN DOORS

WE'RE starting the fitup with probably the most deceptively complicated part of all — the doors. They look simple enough at first glance, but look inside and you'll see that there's an awful lot of individual components. The way that many of them fit in relation to one another is quite critical too.

Taking a door apart is also one of those jobs that leaves you knee-deep in identical-looking (but subtly different) bolts, washers and other fixings and it's all too easy to become totally lost as to what goes where and in what order. I strongly advise keeping all fixings with the part or panel that they're meant to be holding on. Reaching everything can be tricky too. Try sticking to the assembly order shown here — some parts can be fitted earlier but experience has shown that this way seems to give the best accessibility as you go. To take the door apart simply

reverse the process shown — but don't forget that you'll have to drill out the pop-rivets holding the door top bright strip in place.

Before starting the buildup procedure shown here give the door a thorough rust-proofing inside. The MGB Hive spray Waxoyl inside door frames and up to about 5cm (2in) up the skin — but do wear proper breathing gear if you're spraying it in with an airline. Once the Waxoyl has set, poke up through the water drain holes to clear them.

ADJUSTMENTS

AS YOU can see from picture 16 we had a few minor problems setting the door lock to ensure the door position was correct in relation to the rear wing. This sort of thing can take some time to get right, but it's worth persisting with as good panel gaps prove a good indicator of just how a well restoration has been carried out. It's not that unusual for techniques like filing out holes to be required

(I'm told by someone who was there that they often had to do it in the factory), but before you resort to anything like that do make sure that the poor fit isn't caused by something else that can be cured without cutting anything. And once you've ascertained that the holes definitely do need enlarging, take it slowly and don't remove any more metal than is necessary. In our case Neil needed to file out only about 3mm from each hole before the door aligned perfectly with the back wing.

The other adjustment which we haven't shown is setting the door button's clearance. The button operates on the lock via the lock nut shown in picture 10 which needs setting

BODYSHELL BUILDUP

Replacement door key mechanisms mount inside via two discs, one plain and one with two threaded holes. Visualise the door skin in position between the lock barrel outer lip and the plain disc.

Push the lock in normally, then slide the plain disc over and clip the threaded disc on the lock back. Then, by screwing the threaded rods in against the plain disc, the lock's position is fixed.

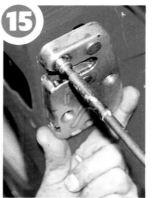

Door lock's position is fixed, so fitting is simply a matter of doing up the three securing bolts — but it'll probably need removing and refitting a few times until you get the knob's clearance correct (see text).

Next, Neil fitted the two internal window runners — after pressing the channel felt into the back one. Front runner is fixed top and bottom now, but leave back runner's lower mount floating at the moment.

Bright strip along top of door is fixed on inner edge by pop-rivets. Then you can fit the draught excluder rubber — which is attached in the traditional way — by U-shaped spring clips in cut-outs in the rubber.

Once this is done, the front piece of channel felt can then be fitted. This can be a little fiddly, but from experience Neil has found that the best way is to start from the top and work your way downwards.

Then bolt the mechanism into place. Each bolt has a plain washer and a split locking washer. Make sure they're both fitted — otherwise the mechanism will probably work loose in service.

Now we can fix the rear window channel bottom end properly. As you can see it attaches via angle bracket. Being in the bottom of the door (and thus susceptible to rust) this usually needs renewing.

Nearly there. Internal handle assembly is held on by a self-tapping screw at the front and an ordinary cheese-head screw (and captive nut) at the back. Feed the two rods into the aperture like this.

o that it's at least 0.8mm (0.03in) off the ck operating arm. This will almost certainly ed resetting if the door's been dismantled, ven if no new parts have been fitted. It's est to adjust this by removing and refitting e lock and reaching inside the door. emoving and refitting the handle will com-

press the mounting gasket which will affect how close to the doorskin the handle sits. And that, in turn will change the plunger clearance.

You can measure the gap with a feeler gauge, but many people find it easier to set the lock by feel. It doesn't matter if the gap is slightly too large if the button's action doesn't

feel sloppy or imprecise. However, it shouldn't be less than the specified figure and the plunger certainly mustn't be in constant contact with the lock.

NEXT ISSUE: completing fitting-up

16 Slight problem. Even when set as far out as it would go, the striker plate held the door too far in. So the plate had to come off for the holes to be filed out slightly. Screw plates behind needed trimming too.

17 Back to the main window surround assembly. External bright strip is attached to rest of frame by two nuts which screw on to studs on bottom of frame. Don't forget gasket between them though.

18 A significant point — fitting the refurbished frame assembly. Here again we found that the locating holes needed a little careful filework before the frame assembly would sit properly in the door.

22 ere's why we left the back channel's bottom end nsecured — so that the door glass can be fed in om the top. Fit glass into the back channel, slide own, and then push into the front channel.

23 Next the window winder mechanism goes in. This bolts to the door frame in two places — at the winder quadrant (where the handle also attaches) and by the plate just above Neil's right hand.

24 Before securing anything, however, get the piece which actually lifts the window connected up. Each of the two pins runs in a channel. If using new components grease the runners, but only very sparingly.

28 low attach each one to its appropriate lever on the ck. Before pushing the rods in, flick the securing ips up above the rods so that once the rods are in lace they can be easily snapped down on to them.

29 If your door's been rebuilt around a new frame don't forget to press these nylon plugs (for the door pull) in place just below the internal handle. Fit them so that the holes are pointing upwards.

30 Final job is to fit the door's internal waterproofing skin. Original fitment varies depending on your car's age, but masking tape is a perfectly satisfactory fixing medium. Cut the handle aperture last of all.

Fitting-up

Our MGB's freshly painted body now gets all dressed up with the interior trim and lots of very shiny bits, reports Peter Simpson

WORKSHOP RATING

TIME REQUIRED 8-10 hours

FITTING EXTERIO

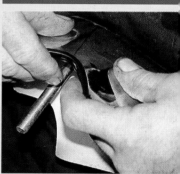

1 Bumpers and overriders are all new, as you'd expect. Overriders bolt to bumpers through triangular spacers. Don't forget this plastic trim around back edge.

4 This fillet plate fills gap between bumper, rear wing and rear panel. It pop-rivets on from underneath. Leave the protective film on while drilling holes.

7 Then mark further dots along the join about 6in apart, drill out, remove the tape then pop-rivet the clips on. MGB Hive recommend completing the front and rear wing fitting before starting on the doors.

WE'RE MOTORING NOW. Our project MGB GT has reached the point where it's starting to look like a real car again rather than a collection of parts spread around the four corners of the workshop. This is the point when a restoration becomes really exciting and you just can't wait to get it on the road.

This issue we're fitting the remaining external brightwork and some soft trim inside, plus we're installing the fuel tank and dropping the front crossmember/suspension assembly ready for overhaul.

There's nothing particularly difficult about any of this — although you'll probably be wary about drilling holes in freshly painted bodywork for the side trims and sticking the vinyl down inside if you haven't done it before. Don't worry, it's easy enough if tackled logically and carefully.

How well you put everything together now will have a major influence on just how good the finished car looks. Don't rush it.

FITTING SIDE TRIMS

LIKE I SAID, drilling holes in a gleaming body panel can be a worry. The nightmare scenario is an out of control drill skidding across the new paintwork. However, with the correct technique it's

BRIGHTWORK

We reused the old bumper brackets — they weren't bent — and they came up like new with a coat of Smoothrite paint. Each of the back brackets goes into a separate cast mount bolted to the rear chassis member.

3 However the front bumper brackets bolt directly to the chassis with captive nuts. The easiest method is to attach them to the bumper first then push through and insert the (new) securing bolts.

The easiest way of fitting the rear bumper bar is to attach the cast mounts (two bolts each) to the chassis first, and then slide the bar, brackets and overriders over the threaded mount ends as one piece.

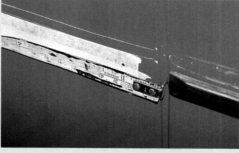

6 The side strip securing clips have to be exactly in line. Attach ½in masking tape with its top edge on the swage line. Then stick another piece of tape on halfway down the first, and mark 1in from panel edge.

Front wing strip fitting is slightly different because there's a captive bolt in the front — there's too much curve for the lugs alone to hold it. Start by taking it finger-tight, then work back pressing strip onto clips.

9 Window surround brightwork is also secured by pop-rivets. The trim comes in three sections — two around the top (the joint's just in front of the rivet gun pictured here) and a wider one underneath the window.

The MGB HIVE

THE PROJECT MGB GT featured on these pages is being restored by the MGB Hive of Parsons Drove, Cambridgeshire (01945 700500).

As well as being a leading supplier of MGB parts, the company undertakes servicing and repairs along with restoration work at their Fenland premises near Wisbech.

The MGB (pictured before restoration work started in late 1994) has now been sold to an enthusiast from Holland. However, our restoration instalments will continue until the November issue, when we'll reveal the completed car in all its glory.

Jobs still to be done:
❖ Underbonnet and electrical fitting-up (September 1996).
❖ Brake restoration (October 1996).
❖ Getting on the road (Nov 1996).

Tools required:
❖ Trolley jack, axle stands
❖ ⁷⁄₁₆, ½, ⁹⁄₁₆ & ⅝in AF spanners or sockets
❖ Pozidriv screwdriver
❖ Copper (or wooden) headed mallet
❖ Pop-rivet gun
❖ Stanley knife (with sharp blade)
❖ Tape measure
❖ Paintbrush and gluebrush (or aerosol glue)

How much would it cost?
An extensive restoration like this where many components have been replaced could cost £10,000 or more, including labour charges, £5000 if you do all the work yourself. You should be able to find a GT suitable for restoration for £500, with a Roadster costing double that.

Sandra Petch of the MGB Hive advises buying a runner that has some sound mechanical components. 'A recent MoT failure is ideal,' she says. 'If it runs you can find out whether items like the gearbox and rear axle are sound. Much better than buying a box of bits you know nothing about.'

Turn over to page 92 for interior trim fitting➔

Fitting-up

nothing to worry about. As our pictures show, this involves using of two pieces of ½in or 80mm masking tape.

Apply the first with its top edge directly along the bottom of the front or rear wing's swage line — in other words so that the tape follows the line exactly but just below it. Ensure the tape goes on smoothly and without bunching or sticking to itself.

Then apply another length of tape halfway down it and drill holes for the pop-rivets. The tape will protect the paint from 'wandering drill' damage and save you the cost of a resprayed panel.

INTERIOR TRIM

WE'RE sticking four pieces of vinyl to the body. Two of these are to fill the gaps between carpet and trim panels, one is to fill the gap between the rear side trim and rear side window surround, and the final one's to cover the centre door pillar. Apart from the last mentioned, there's some flexibility in the positioning of them all — only a small part of what you're fitting will show. However, I recommend trial-fitting the adjacent trim piece(s) first — to make sure no body colour is showing through. At least one edge of each of them will be tucked under a rubber surround — make sure they're fitted with enough material spare at the edge(s) to go right round the lip. If you don't do this the vinyl may work its way out in time.

Any good contact adhesive for bonding vinyl and metal is suitable. Ask at your local trim supplier or a hardware shop.

The rest of the interior fit-up is straigh forward. Things like dropping in pre-cut pieces of carpet or pressing pre-made sof trim panels over don't really need demon strating. You would normally do all this a little later on in the buildup — after all th mechanical components, wiring and con trol cables have been fitted. However, the interior bits shown being done here all de have to go on at this stage.

CROSSMEMBER OUT

THE LAST three photographs in our sequence show how to drop the front cros member for front suspension overhaul. You wouldn't normally do this — it's easi

FITTING FUEL TANK AND INTERIOR TRIM

1 Neil Fincham painted the new petrol tank with Smoothrite to improve appearance and help preserve it. When dry he stuck four 2mm rubber strips across (not along) pressings to avoid chafing body.

2 After fitting the gauge sender unit (don't forget sealing rubber) the tank was lifted into place. Tank bolts to the loadspace floor — support it here while you push the setscrews through from the top.

3 Now wash your hands for some inside work. Th centre door pillar has to be covered with stuck on black vinyl. Use contact adhesive and tuck the edges of the vinyl right round the lips on either side

5 Door draught excluder comes 'off the roll' and has to be cut to length. Cut the end off at 45 degrees (inner edge shortest) and press the end right up into the corner.

6 Then work round, making sure that the seal go right down, on and over the top edges of the stuck-on vinyl. At the corners a few modest taps fr a copper-headed mallet will help it sit right...

8 Neil's next job was to fit door interior trim panel. It's a clip-on fit, but there's a small cross-headed screw (and washer) in each bottom corner — you'll need to drill holes for these in the trim.

9 The door waist rail/trim pad assembly goes on next — ours was deemed good enough to reuse after a thorough clean. It's held on by chrome crosshead screws front and back.

10 Sill carpet section is glued over sill. Tuck top edge up to the door draught excluder. Vinyl piece mentioned in caption 4 is visible on the left — the door rubber's trapping its top edge down

undertake in-service repairs under the wheelarch. However, this approach is recommended during a full rebuild, partly because it gives better access (for our photography as well as rebuilding the kingpins), but mainly because the removed crossmember can be shot-blasted and checked for corrosion.

Most MGB crossmembers are perfectly sound, but I've seen a few cases of serious rot around the coil spring top mounts and stress-cracks around the shock absorber and steering rack mounts.

Once blasted, checked and repaired if necessary, the crossmember can be given a good coat of paint so that it looks as smart as the rest of the car. Which, as you can see from the pictures below, it certainly isn't when removed from the car...

Copies of these issues are available from our Back Issues department, details page 3.

Copies of the February, March, April, Spring, October and December 1995 issues along with Spring and May 1996 are available from our back issues department (01858 468888), priced £2.50. Unfortunately due to popular demand the remainder have sold out, but reprints are available from the editorial office (Judy Scott, 01733 237111, ex 5666).

A *Practical Classics* MGB GT restoration book is planned for publication before Christmas. The *Practical Classics MGB Uprating & Bodyshell Rebuild* book is available from Kelsey Publishing (0181 658 3531) price £10.95.

Two strips also go on the top of the sill to fill gaps between carpet and side trim panel. One goes here, the other's just below the bottom door edge. Again, the vinyl must fold right over the lip.

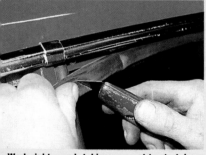

Work right round, taking care not to stretch or bunch the rubber. When you're back at the top left corner cut off at 45 degrees again so that the two ends meet. This rubber is not glued on.

Don't put the glue away yet, there's another backing strip to fit — along the bottom edge of the rear window aperture. It fits behind door rubber and (when it's fitted) the rear window rubber.

FRONT AXLE OUT

1 Now more mechanical work to finish off this time — dropping the front suspension. Apart from the anti-roll bar, it's mounted on a main crossmember. Start by removing the anti-roll bar brackets.

2 Then disconnect steering and brakes (we'd already dealt with these), put a trolley jack under the crossmember as in our heading shot and slowly undo the four crossmember securing nuts.

3 As the crossmember starts to drop away from the car lower the jack to take up the strain. Then, when it's completely free, lower the jack right down and drag the complete assembly out. Ideally you'll need help for this.

Finally, over the next three episodes the more sharp-eyed among you may spot a few continuity inconsistencies in the background. This time, for example, some electrical components and part of the loom can be seen fitted, though we haven't yet covered electrics.

The reason for this is quite simple. The MGB Hive has sold 'our' car, and to meet the delivery deadline the work you'll be reading about from now on had to be completed in a couple of weeks! Consequently,

up to four different technicians from the MGB Hive were working on different parts of the car at the same time.

However, we've taken care to ensure that the order of operations shown is the one normally adopted on less-hectic projects and that's the one you should follow at home. Apart from engine installation (which is a straightforward reversal of removal — see December 1995) we'll be covering key parts of the underbonnet and electrical installation next time.

Nearly

REWIRING REWIRING

WORKSHOP RATING

TIME REQUIRED
2 FULL WEEKENDS

C C C C C

Peter Simpson reports as our MGB gets a new wiring loom, heater box, pedal assembly and front suspension rebuild

A S OUR MGB project car steams rapidly towards completion, we're looking at two major tasks — rewiring and the front suspension rebuild — plus reassembling the pedal box and building and installing the heater.

Rewiring a car is a job many people are frightened of, and with good reason. There's a lot to it, and it's easy to get wrong if you're not careful. We had two things on our side — the MGB Hive have done hundreds of rewires so know where everything should go, and we were working with a substantially stripped shell...

GET THE RIGHT LOOM...

MGB WIRING looms changed a lot over the years as the cars were updated. It's therefore absolutely vital to quote year and chassis number when ordering a ready-made loom. Even then, it's unlikely that you'll get a new loom that matches your old one exactly — replacement looms usually include wiring for all commonly-specified accessories.

The most important fitting tip is to be methodical. Start by fitting as many of the panel-mounted under-bonnet electrical components as possible — especially the fusebox, regulator and others with lots of connections in and out. Don't unplug the old loom from these during dismantling — cut it instead, so that a short length of coloured wire remains on each terminal. These will be invaluable as tracers and

prove exactly what goes where. Remove the main loom-end multipins (where the different sections of the loom are joined) in the same way. This 'tracer tag' method of identifying what goes where works very well, and is strongly recommended — especially if you're new to MGBs and/or vehicle wiring.

Now lay the new loom out as close as possible to where it'll end up. Put the under-dash loom for example (usually the most complex bit) on the floor directly underneath. Then, looking at the old and new, work out what goes where and plan how you're going to install it.

Where wiring passes through a panel aperture it can usually be put in one way round only. Even then, you sometimes have to fit the multipin that's on the other side of the hole from the rest of the loom after installation. You can usually take it that if the new loom comes with multipin(s) loose they have to be fitted after installation.

Plan the order in which you're going to connect things up, too. That's particularly important in inaccessible areas such as the under-dash area. Generally, it's best to start with the bits that are farthest in and then work out. Then, and only then, you can start work. Remove each old tracer tag one at a time, replacing it with a connection from your new loom. If you later have to take that lead off again, refit the tracer. Don't rely on memory. If you work this way and take your time the whole job will be remarkably simple.

1 Where loom passes through body apertures a rubber grommet stops it chafing. Fit this to the wiring first — it' difficult to push the wires through an already-fitted gromme

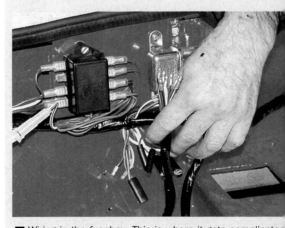

3 Wiring in the fusebox. This is where it gets complicated Follow wiring diagram carefully for your year of car and start with the components with the most connections.

5 Use anti-roll bar bushes to protect the underbody wiring loom where it passes through the central crossmember The rest of the loom is attached by tabs underneath.

eady

The MGB HIVE

The project MGB GT featured on these pages is being restored by the MGB Hive of Parsons Drove, Cambridgeshire (01945 700500).

As well as being a leading supplier of MGB parts, the company undertakes servicing and repairs along with restoration work at their Fenland premises near Wisbech. The MGB restoration will continue until the November 1996 issue, when we'll reveal the completed car in all its glory.

REWIRING REWIRING

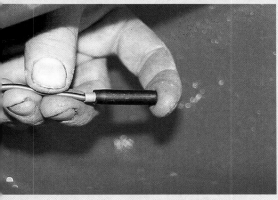

Fit bullet connectors as soon as a wire's been installed. That way you won't get a short if someone reconnects the battery. Use known-name connectors — cheap ones break.

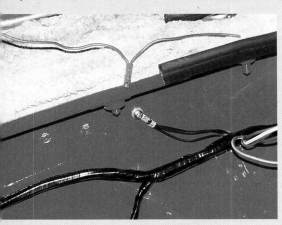

Black wires are invariably earths and where there's a looped connection like this it has to be screwed onto something — usually the shell. Ensure connection is tight.

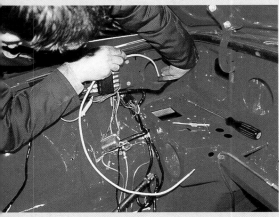

Fit accelerator cable's outer into its bulkhead seating. Pop a piece of insulating tape round the inner cable's other end stop it coming out while you're connecting up the pedal.

HEATER AND PEDAL BOX

ASSEMBLY is precisely as shown in the picture sequence, right, and over the page. The MGB heater radiator isn't wonderful — it's prone to clogging which results in even less output than the hardly-wonderful normal. So give yours a thorough flush-out at the very least, and consider renewal if it looks at all doubtful.

FRONT SUSPENSION OVERHAUL

OUR OTHER main task is one that's often needed on MGBs — a front suspension/swivel pin (king-pin) overhaul. 'In service' this would normally be done on the vehicle. However, as we saw last time, dropping the crossmember is straightforward and enabled us to clean and paint it to match the rest of the car.

Wherever the job's tackled, though, it's vital that the coil spring is removed and refitted carefully. Even a part-compressed spring flying out of position can cause very serious injury. As you can see, the MGB Hive have a homemade and very effective tool designed for controlled removal and fitting of coil springs.

However, a good trolley jack (but not a scissor jack) will do just as well. Proceed as follows. With the vehicle raised and firmly supported on axle stands, position the jack underneath the lower spring pan so that it's taking the pan's weight — but make sure it's not lifting the vehicle. Undo the lower pan bolts carefully. Then slowly lower the jack, allowing the spring pan to come away from the wishbone arms. As it drops, the coil spring will gradually lose its tension but with you controlling it.

That apart, the job is as shown in the picture sequence (over the page). Make sure that all components which should move in relation to each other are able to do so but without excess slackness. We fitted new coil springs — check length of yours against table and renew both if either spring is outside these limits.

PEDAL BOX ASSEMBLY

Neil Fincham wire-brushed the old pedal box to remove loose rust. He then repainted it in Hammerite, and as you can see it came up very well. It's secured to the bulkhead by eight bolts going into captive nuts — and don't forget to fit the soft gasket.

Get an assistant to push the pedals up from inside the car while you slide in the spindle pin. Don't forget the washers and spacer between the pedals and the smaller washers at each end.

After fitting the clutch and brake master cylinders (unfortunately the original square-type MGB brake master cylinders aren't available) Neil fitted and screwed down the front cover with four self-tappers.

Turn the page for the front suspension rebuild →

COIL SPRING FREE LENGTHS

Early 18G & 18GA models 9.9in (251.4mm)
Early 18GB models 9.1in +/- 0.06in (231mm +/- 1.5mm)
Roadster from chassis no 293446 10.20 +/- 0.06in (259.08 +/- 1.5mm)
GT from chassis number 296196 9.32 +/- 0.06in (237 +/- 1.5mm) (Change both springs if either is more than 10 percent shorter than these figures)

TORQUE WRENCH SETTINGS

Spring pan nuts and screws: 22lb/ft (30Nm)
Shock absorber bolts: 43-45lb/ft (58-61Nm)
Crossmember to body: 54-56lb/ft (73-76Nm)

TOOLS REQUIRED

Wiring:
❖ Electrical pliers
❖ Electrical connection crimper
❖ Simple multimeter (not essential but makes it easier to track down any mistakes!)

Front suspension:
❖ Trolley jack and good axle stands (see our test on page158)
❖ ¹⁄₁₆, ½, ⁹⁄₁₆ and ⅝AF ring spanners
❖ Straight and pozidriv screwdrivers
❖ Good quality grease gun
❖ Copper-headed hammer

FRONT SUSPENSION REBUILD

1 If starting with a fully-dismantled front suspension beam the first job is to bolt the bottom swivel joint. New bolts and nylocs are recommended for all the work that follows.

2 Shock absorber bolts onto crossmember. Before fitting, wo▪ arm fully up and down half a dozen times. Shock absorber bump stop (on right) was renewed — they are often missing.

4 Treat both surfaces of the lower wishbone inner bushes with copper-based grease — it prevents them from seizing up and makes them much easier to press into place.

5 Pop the rear wishbone on and then bolt the spring pan up▪ to it. These pans are susceptible to distortion and fatigue cracks — renew it if there's any doubt about its condition.

7 After fitting and split-pinning the lower joint's fulcrum pin (so the nut's at the front) fasten the front arm to the spring pan. Outer fixing (shown here) incorporates anti-roll bar arm.

8 Meet the MGB Hive's secret weapon for removal/fitting of c▪ springs. This MUST be done correctly — use a good trolley jack as explained in main text if suspension's still on vehicle.

9 And here it is in action. The spring's slid in and as it's compressed by the jacking action the chain is pulled tight to keep the spring in. Make sure it's seated correctly.

10 As soon as the spring's compressed sufficiently slide the top pin through the top joint and bushes to box the job u▪ Note that the shock absorber arms have been parted slightly.

Kingpins and bushes can be renewed but doing so involves reaming the new bushes to size, so it's easier to buy and install a complete exchange stub-axle assembly like this.

Now put the front arm on, but don't bolt it to the spring pan yet. Fit the swivel pin assembly first, complete with the end washers, sealing rings and some copper grease.

The MGB HIVE

NEXT ISSUE Brake overhaul/fitting-up

● Copies of these issues are available from our Back Issues department (01858 435337).
● Copies of the February, March, April, Spring, October and December 1995 issues along with Spring and May 1996 are available from our back issues department (01858 468888), priced £2.50. Unfortunately due to popular demand the remainder have sold out, but reprints are available from the editorial office (Judy Scott, 01733 237111, ex 5666)
● A *Practical Classics* MGB GT restoration book is planned for publication before Christmas. The *Practical Classics MGB Uprating & Bodyshell Rebuild* book is available from Kelsey Publishing (0181 658 3531) price £10.95.

HEATER BOX ASSEMBLY

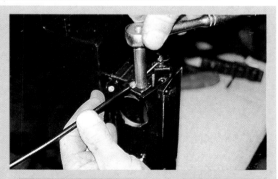

LEFT: MGB heater matrix often gets clogged so was renewed. To fit, first wrap its edge and both pipe outlets in heat-resistant foam. Most domestic furnishing foams are far from heat-resistant.

RIGHT: the control flap is in a separate section that goes underneath the main box. Tip: it's a lot, lot easier to connect the 'flap' end of the control cable before the heater box goes in.

LEFT: then close the box by fitting the top. The two halves are held together by sprung clips around the body. Again, a coat of Hammerite bought the old heater box up like new.

RIGHT: to fit the heater box assembly without scratching your nice new paintwork, go in at an angle first with the offside lower than nearside and then straighten as the box goes down.

Fixing the brakes

Just one job left before our MGB can take to the road again, but it's an important one! Peter Simpson reports

The MGB HIVE

The project MGB GT featured on these pages is being restored by the MGB Hive of Parson Drove, Cambridgeshire (01945 700500). As well as being a leading supplier of MGB parts, the company undertakes servicing and repairs along with restoration work at their Fenland premises near Wisbech.

The restoration will come to an end in the next issue, when we'll reveal the completed car in all its glory.

TOOLS REQUIRED

❖ ½in AF & ⅜in AF spanners and sockets (two tools of each size needed) and 28mm socket
❖ Molegrips (large)
❖ Brake adjusting spanner, brake pipe spanner and brake pipe clamps
❖ Engineering hammer and soft-faced mallet
❖ Torque wrench, screwdriver and pliers
❖ Gunson's Eezibleed

TORQUE WRENCH SETTINGS

Caliper securing bolts 40-45lb/ft (54-61Nm)
Bearing retaining nut 40-70lb/ft (54-94Nm)

PERMITTED TOLERANCES

Front wheel bearing endfloat 0.002-0.004in (0.05-0.12mm)
Maximum disc runout 0.006in (0.15mm)

BELIEVE it or not, we've reached the penultimate part of our MGB restoration epic. Just one significant job remains — overhauling and fitting up the braking system. As you might tackle this job without doing a full car rebuild, we're going into the whole strip and rebuild process as you might do it at home.

Spares for an MGB braking system are plentiful, so all hydraulic components were replaced. This wasn't just because our car is being rebuilt as-new — it's quicker, therefore cost-effective. New cylinders are £15 and an exchange caliper is £36.

Brake hoses and pipes were renewed too. Like most restorers, the MGB Hive uses copper brake pipes, which have two benefits. First, they don't rust, and secondly they keep their looks longer — important for a car as well-finished as our B. Being more flexible than steel, copper piping needs fixing to the car in more places — use the extra clips that come with the kit.

Since all the old system was being renewed we just cut through the pipes, which is easier than trying to undo rusty unions. Avoid bending the old pipes more than necessary though — you can then use them as patterns for shaping the new ones.

FRONT BRAKES

THE overhaul procedure is as shown in the pictures. Brake manufacturers will say that you should use a dial test indicator (or DTI) to check each brake disc's side-to-side

movement (or runout) in relation to the hub, but if you're careful about cleaning the mating surfaces and torquing the bolt properly (in diagonal sequence) you won' be far out. Perfectionists may object, but that's what those in the trade do.

Unlike most cars, the MGB's front whee bearings aren't adjusted until the it 'feels right — the centre nut must tighten to a predetermined torque. Admittedly the range is wide, but that's so you can line u the castellated nut with the split pin hole in the stub axle. Shims between inner and outer race control the bearing's actual play; the setting-up procedure is as follow

Tighten the centre nut until the bearing locks to ensure everything's seated proper! Then undo the nut, removing the washer and outer bearing. Refit the bearing after inserting shims between it and the inner to give correct end-float when the nut is fi ted to the right torque. Ideally this too should be measured with a DTI, but it isn essential if you're careful. Look how thic a 0.002-0.004in feeler gauge is. That's how much side-to-side movement there should be — in other words hardly any!

Of course none of this is necessary if you're reusing the old bearings, though this is often a false economy. Naturally ou car got a new set. Don't forget to change the outer running surfaces (the bits insid the hub) as well — there's handy cutouts push them out. Press the new ones in using a drift or suitable-sized socket as shown, taking care that they go in straigh and the running surfaces aren't damaged

1 Start by clamping the brake hose like this to prevent fluid from escaping when the caliper is removed. Make sure you use proper brake pipe clamps for this — never a pair of Mole grips!

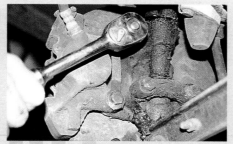

2 Then after removing the pads and their retaining pins, knock back the locking tabs and undo the ⁵⁄₁₆AF bolts holding the caliper on to the stub axle. Pull caliper off and unscrew from hose.

3 To remove the disc/wheel bearing assembly, prise the bearing dust cover off, extract the split pin (always use a new one on reassembly) and undo the 28mm (and probably tight) centre nut.

4 You can then pull the complete disc assembly off. As it comes away the outer bearing race will come out. Underneath there will probably be one or more shim washers. These are used to set the bearing's end-float.

5 Disc is held on bearing housing by four nuts and bolts — ⁵⁄₁₆AF again. Air power makes life easy, but whatever method you use the bolts aren't captive so need holding with a spanner.

6 Check the bearing housing mating surface carefully for dirt and corrosion. The new disc must sit straight on this — just one small speck of dirt here can throw the disc edge runout beyond acceptable tolerance.

7 It is best to always renew wheelbearings in sets, including the running surfaces. New ones can be tapped in (if you're very careful) using a socket big enough to sit right round the bearing's edge but small enough to slide down into housing.

8 Clean new disc with brake cleaner — they're coated in protective film to stop corrosion in storage. Original disc fixing bolts can be reused but MUST be tightened diagonally to correct torque.

9 Refit disc (after checking backplate for damage) using new bearings if necessary — otherwise clean and regrease the originals. Then tighten the centre nut using procedure given in the text.

10 Attach new hose to car piping first. Then, not forgetting copper washer, screw new caliper on, holding the hose still to avoid twisting. Give hose a quick nip (⁵⁄₁₆in AF spanner) to finally tighten.

11 Always use a new locking tab with the new caliper — a decent reconditioned unit should come with one anyway. Caliper securing bolts should be torqued to recommended setting.

12 Apply a little copper-based grease to the back of the new pads before fitting them, making sure you don't get any on the friction side. The grease will dampen unnecessary movement between the pad and piston, therefore eliminating brake squeal.

REAR BRAKES

HERE too the procedure is as shown — the only further explanation needed is initial adjustment. This should be done after bleeding the system with the handbrake cable disconnected from each wheel. Adjust up until the drum cannot be moved but the adjuster has slight side-to-side movement, indicating that the flats of the adjuster screw are on the pistons. Then back off a quarter or, if necessary, half a turn only. If all's well the drum should spin freely but give maximum braking efficiency.

Now reconnect the handbrake. Adjust the brass nut under the lever until the

Turn the page for the rear brake rebuild →

REAR BRAKES REAR BRAKES REAR BRAKES

1 Spray brake adjuster nut with oil and back off as far as possible to make drum removal easier. If still tight, try tapping drum ONTO axle with a soft-faced mallet — this should jolt it free.

2 Unclip the top spring, then lever the shoes out of contact with the cylinder and handbrake mechanism. Note which way round they are — drum should pass over the lining-free section last when moving forwards.

3 Rear brake adjusters are prone to seizure on MGBs. Remove adjuster pistons and work the adjuster in and out. You'll have to fit a new adjuster if the old one can't be freed off satisfactorily.

4 After removing brake pipe, release the wheel cylinder by levering this spring clip off. It'll probably break but use a new one on reassembly anyway. There's no need to remove bleed nipple.

5 MGB GT (left) and Roadster (right) wheel cylinders aren't the same! Look at locating pins next to bleed nipple. However this is an ID point only — important point is that bore sizes are different too.

6 Here's a handy tip which will come in useful on reassembly. If you grip the drum mounting plate like this, the Mole grips will hold the cylinder tightly in place while you fit retaining spring clip on the back!

7 Fitting new shoes. Set adjuster as far out as possible. Then fit top spring behind the shoes with its hooked ends bending out into the slots and pull the shoes around the adjuster and into its slots.

8 Bottom's a bit more complicated. Handbrake arm goes into back shoe and long arm from spring sits on top like this. Smaller spring (being stretched here) goes in small hole in handbrake arm.

9 Before refitting the drum, coat its mating flange with copper grease (not too much — excess may get on to the linings). It will probably be you who will have to take it all off again next time!

brakes are fully on when the handle's up four or five notches. New cables can stretch, but once settled rarely need adjustment.

BLEEDING

ONCE the system's together you need to bleed fluid through, which is tricky using the 'pedal pumping' method. I use a Gunson's Eezibleed device (about £13 from accessory shops), which pressurises the whole system. Just fill it with fluid, connect to both the system and a semi-inflated tyre (10-15psi), then open each bleed nipple in turn, starting farthest from the master cylinder and working back.

Only the servo might not bleed this way. If the pedal stays spongy, re-bleed with the engine running — that can help fluid flow

The **MGB HIVE**
NEXT ISSUE finally, on the road again

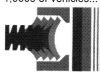

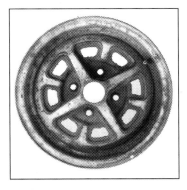

Finished!

COH 500K

At last, 25 issues after coverage started, our restoration project MGB GT is back on the road. Peter Simpson drives the finished car and reckons it was worth the wait

The author takes our restored MGB for some fen fun. MGB GTs are a bit cramped if, like Peter, you're over 6ft tall. Controls are taut, precise, and work as they should.

...springs, kingpins and lever–arm front shock ...rbers give MGB plenty of roll on cornering, ...s–new suspension improves matters a lot.

Underbonnet is superb and correct as possible in detail. Black block was typical seventies BL corporatism — MGs used to have red engines.

BACK in the September 1994 issue, we introduced a very rusty, incomplete, matt red MGB GT. Despite looking like a no-hoper COH ...K was not beyond salvation — ...structure was judged restor... ...e and *Practical Classics* had ...en on projects much worse ...n this in the past. So over the ...owing two years we systemati... ...y turned that rusty wreck into ... highly presentable example. ...s the back-numbers listing ...rleaf shows, in the course of ... project we've demonstrated ...w to do just about every ...on an MGB. We've also ...d to divide the cover... ...into tasks which can ...ackled separately on a ...nning rebuild' basis. ...ns like fitting the front ...gs, repairing the ...er wings, ...ewing the ...cooler ...el and all ...mechani- ...work have ...n covered as ...-contained ...ts. However, ... isn't always pos-

sible — for example you can't do a proper sill job on an MGB without repairing the front bulkhead and removing part of the rear wing, the latter being likely to reveal rot in the wheelarches, rear panel and boot floor.

WHAT'S IT COST?

WELL, since the project was a 'restoration for resale' job the precise cost of the job comes under the heading 'confidential business information' and cannot be published. However, the car was sold for around £10,000 which, according

...it lives and moves! Our MGB ...riving through typical ...oridgeshire fenland landscape ...h, come to think of it, isn't unlike ...nd where it now resides.

THIS IS WHAT WE DID...

Both floorpans needed renewing as far in as the transmission tunnel. Although the central crossmember is a one-piece pressing it's usually cut in the middle and each half renewed separately.

There's a lot more to MGB sills than meets the eye! As you can see, there are no less than four separate longitudinal members. This picture also shows new floorpan and centre crossmember.

Front inner wings were repaired rather than completely renewed. The key here is to cut back until you reach solid metal — this will probably mean removing much more rot than you were expecting...

Boot floor usually needs completely renewing, and ours was no exception. Both rear wings, and the outer half of the wheelarches needed replacing too, along with most of the chassis legs behind the wheelarch.

The back panel needed replacing too, but this has to be done after the boot floor as the panel is used as a positioning reference. Good-quality replacement panels make work like this a lot easier.

Lucky Practical Classics reader Richard Van Tunen from Holland gets the feel of our MGB GT — which became his MGB GT about an hour after this picture was taken...

to The MGB Hive's Sandra Petch just about covered their parts and labour costs — in equal proportions. If you replace everything that you can irrespective of condition, the parts bill will go way over that. Unless you have limitless finance then you must assess everything and consider reusing it where possible.

Obviously, anything which will detract from the finished project should be renewed. But it's surprising how often things like glass, metal internal components and aluminium brightwork can be cleaned up like new using just elbow grease and proprietory cleaning products.

When restoring a car like an MGB for which spares availability is superb it's easy to pick up a suppliers catalogue and order, new, everything you can see for the part you're tackling. I strongly advise resisting the temptation to do this until you've looked over the whole car and

know what really does need doing, otherwise your project will end up costing far more than you've budgeted for.

Incidentally, even on a car like an MGB, you can't get every single part needed to build one from scratch. Bits which don't deteriorate in service such as brackets, heater ducts, seat runners and so on are not normally available new as there isn't any demand for them, so the only place you'll get replacements is from a scrap car.

ON THE ROAD

ENOUGH of this — you want to know what the car finally felt like to drive! Having seen first-hand the work and care that went into this particular MGB I was, naturally, a little apprehensive about this bit. I even wiped my feet before getting in...

On the move the first thing I noticed was that characteristic MGB engine burble, accompanied by the equally typical slight tappet noise on pulling away.

The second thing I noticed was how clearly I could hear both those sounds without all the trim rattles and other extraneous sounds which you normally get from Bs that have seen a little life — even low-mileage original ones. And, as usual with new project cars, the doors needed a fairly heavy pull shut — this will change, however, once the new rubbers settle in.

Acceleration seemed rapid and progressive (considering the car was nowhere near run in) and it was a novel experience to be driving a B on which all the controls and switches felt taut and unworn; the choke knob stayed out when pulled, the light and headlamp switches worked with a reassuring click and even the heater knobs turned smoothly and positively.

MGBs aren't the ultimate sports cars around corners — its predecessor the

Which one would you buy — our completed car alongside some awaiting rebuild in The MGB Hive's 'field'? Richard Van Tunen was in no doubt.

MGA was miles better in this respect — and ours is no exception as you can see from the cornering shots. Saying that, the roll didn't seem anything like as bad as I'd anticipated — maybe because our car was put together so well.

I didn't do any top speed or acceleration tests — these don't tell you much anyway when a car's this new — but I did take it up to the legal limit on a straight section of dual carriageway. At 70mph the car remained as smooth and taut as it had been at 30, and there were no nasty trim rattles or other distractions. Even the speedo needle remained rock-steady. The brakes then bought the car to a smooth, definite stop without wander or squeal — and they probably aren't yet bedded in.

In short, the whole car felt right — I'm not quite old enough to have driven chrome-bumpered MGBs when they were new, but I'm pretty sure that driving this one was as close to the experience as anyone in 1996 is likely to get. I loved it! *Practical Classics* reader Richard Van Tunen agreed. Having seen this series, h

❖ Copies of the February, March, April, Spring, October and December 1995 issues along with Spring to October 1996 are available from our back issues department (01858 468888), priced £2.50. Unfortunately due to popular demand the remainder have sold out, but reprints are available from the editorial office (Judy Scott, 01733 237111, extension 5666)
❖ A *Practical Classics* MGB GT restoration book is planned for publication before Christmas. The *Practical Classics MGB Uprating & Bodyshell Rebuild* book is available from Kelsey Publishing (0181 658 3531) price £10.95.

Front wings bolt on, making fitting and alignment easier. Sill ends run under front and rear wings, so you have to remove the fronts, cutting away rear's lower edge and welding a repair section in afterwards.

THIS IS WHAT WE DID...

Engine was left in until after sills were done as alignment's easier with its weight bearing on the front end. As engine and gearbox were both going to be fully overhauled they came out as one unit.

me over from Holland to inspect e car and ended up driving it back ome the same day. Some may think s sad that such a fine example has ne abroad. I'm not that concerned ough — to me, the important ing is that the latest in a long line completed *Practical Classics* pro- ct cars has gone to someone who early appreciates old cars and tends to look after, use and enjoy is one. Good luck Richard, and do ep in touch.

Finally, my heartfelt thanks go to everyone at the MGB Hive for making this such an enjoyable project to follow. Not just proprietors Nigel and Sandra Petch but also Neil Fincham who did the metalwork, Norman Hatcher who did the engine and gearbox rebuilds and Neil Watton (paintwork). Everyone in the MGB Hive's team is a real expert in their field of MGB restoration, and working with such a knowledgeable and enthusiastic team of professionals has been a real pleasure.

Like many restorers, the MGB Hive have machining and some engine assembly work done outside but our motor was built up in house by the very skilled and experienced Norman Hatcher.

Norman (who, as you can see, doesn't like lending his tools) also rebuilt the main gearbox. A service exchange overdrive unit was used though — rebuilding these requires specialist skill and equipment.

The team that made it happen (back row). The two in front are the buyer and our Peter.

The car was very thoroughly rustproofed at all stages so that hopefully its second life will be longer than its first. Here Neil's doing the business inside driver's door.

Classic Car Insurance

110